Beti Bachao, Beti Padao: Current Perspective

BETI BACHAO, BETI PADAO
Current Perspective

Asha Kiran

SUN SHINE BOOKS
NEW DELHI-110002

Beti Bachao, Beti Padao: Current Perspective

First Edition : 2019

ISBN : 978-93-80920-77-1

Published by

SUN SHINE BOOKS

4760-4761,2nd Floor,
23 Ansari Road, Daryaganj,
New Delhi, Delhi 110002

PRINTED IN INDIA

Contents

Preface

Beti Bachao, Beti Padhao is a government social scheme launched by the Prime Minister Narendra Modi in order to address the gender imbalance and discrimination against girl child in the Indian society. This scheme was launched by the Prime Minister on 22nd of January in 2015 at Panipat, Haryana on Thursday. This scheme is to aware people about the importance of girls in the society. It is to increase awareness among common people to save the lives of girl child by completely removing the female foeticide. People should celebrate the birth of their girl child and educate them with full responsibility as they do for their boy child.

Prime Minister Narendra Modi has launched a scheme for girls named Beti Bachao Beti Padhao in order to save the girl child and educate the girl child all over the India. The programme was launched on 22nd of January, Thursday in 2015 at Panipat,. This scheme was launched especially in Haryana as this state has lowest female sex ratio (775 girls/1000 boys) all over the country. It has been effectively implemented in hundred districts across the country to improve the status of girls. 12 districts (Ambala, Kurukshetra, Rewari, Bhiwani, Mahendergarh, Sonepat, Jhajjar, Rohtak, Kaithal, Panipat, Karnal, and Yamuna Nagar) have been chosen from the Haryana state itself because of having low child sex ratio.

In order to improve the status of girls and give them importance, Haryana Government celebrates an event named Beti ki Lohri on January 14. The purpose of launching Beti Bachao Beti Padhao scheme is to make girls independent socially and financially using their proper rights and higher education. It helps in improving the awareness among common public and improving the efficiency of welfare services given to women. If we have a sight on latest census report of 2011, we see a continuous decrease in the female child sex ratio (of age group 0-6 years) from last some decades.

Literally meaning 'Educate the Girl Child, Save the Girl Child' the Beti Padhao, Beti Bachao Scheme is an ambitious scheme of the Government of India which is intended to generate massive awareness, improvement of quality of welfare services for females and helping them (girls and women) access these services better.

Introduced in October of 2014, the Beti Bachao, Beti Padhao Scheme goes on to address the declining Child Sex Ratio in the country. The scheme is being rolled out through pan-India campaigns with focus on 100 worst-performing districts in terms of CSR. It is a joint initiative of three important Central Government ministries – the Ministry of Women and Child Development, Ministry of Health and Family Welfare and Ministry of Human Resource Development.

This is a reference book. All the matter is just compiled and edited in nature, taken from the various sources which are in public domain.

This book narrates the status and trends of save the girl child and girl education in the context of global economic reforms in India.

—Editor

1

Introduction

This year Jan 2015 will witness the change in lives of countless girl child and women. The pet project launched by Prime Minister Shri Narender Modi "Beti bachao beti Padhao" (BBBP) Yojana (save daughter, educate daughter) to save and empower the girl child is making waves all over the nation. This major inter-ministerial initiative of the Government of India bringing together Ministries, institutions and civil societies, though not a drastic change yet, the results are positive on the scheme. The scheme will have focussed intervention and multi-section action in almost 100 districts with low Child Sex Ratio (CSR).

"The village that succeeds in attaining a balanced sex ratio will be awarded Rs 1 crore"this strong incentive will reduce the declining CSRensuring that the girl child gets equal opportunities to shine.

Finance minister Mr.Arun Jaitley in his Budget speech announced that the government would focus on campaigns to sensitise the citizens of this country towards the concerns of the girl child and women.

He also included that this process must begin early and therefore the school curriculum must have a separate chapter on the core subject of gender equality. The financial figures to assist the issue include Rs. 50 crore for testing a scheme for safety of women on Public Road Transport by The Ministry of Road Transport and Highways. Additionally, Rs.150 crore will be spent by Ministry of Home Affairs to increase the safety of women in large cities. From the Nirbhaya fund, there is a proposal to set up Crisis Management Centres this year, in all districts of the capital, Delhi. The centres will be set up in all Government and Private Hospitals.

From the workshops conducted of District Collectors held in Chandigarh, Guwahati and Delhi till now, the suggestions that have come out are

- More stringent Anti-Dowry Act
- Preventing Child marriage through compulsory registration of marriages
- Celebrating the birth of the girl child
- Emphasis on the education of the girl child for their empowerment. This will make the Zila Panchayats prominent in implementing and monitoring BBBP.
- Economic incentives as a motivation were also suggested by the members.

The essential fact to be noted here is that allottingfunds and schemes alone will not work wonders. The laws have to be amended, the culprits have to be vigorously punished, the ones involved in the practice of sex determination and sex selective abortion should be punished severely, and the government has to talk tough so that doctors do not indulge in this malpractice.

Personally according to me, a connection first with all has to be established with the society at large.

This will make the citizens more sensitive and will be able to relate themselves better to how and what the ill-treated girl child feels like. Working towards the BBBP Yojana, the latest advertisements in the Television are fantastically making the audience more human in this perspective. The campaigns are boosting the morals of people and helping the unspoken to reach out. If you want results, dedicated efforts have to be clubbed with the monetary incentives.

The associated problems in bringing up the girl child, her marriage expenses, Dowry system and discrimination in the society have to be talked out more often so that the citizens, showcase more responsible behaviour or even out of shame think twice before indulging themselves in such crimes or acts of violence. There definitely are families who care exclusively for their girl child. It's just that the issues have to be talked smartly and encourage the future parents with a positive role.

The immediate issues to be tackled now are,

1. Awareness on gender equality
2. Education for women
3. Medical aid and health issues
4. Safety in public transport system
5. Women safety cells
6. Campaigns on sensitization towards women and children
7. Cybercrime cells
8. Crisis Management centre's
9. Awards for role models, parents and other categories

These initiatives will provide a pathway to the young generation. Prime Minister said 'Beta Beti ek saman'; this should be everyone's mantra. Isn't this marvellous? Well, Yes! This is a wonderful phase in the life of each girl suffering out there to come out of the shell.

WHY BETI BACHAO, BETI PADHAO SCHEME ?

The latest census of 2011 reveals a declining trend in CSR in the age group of 0 to 6 years, the figure for girls having gone down to 919 per 1,000 boys from 927 in the 2001. The practice of aborting female foetus has become more rampant with the availability of modern diagnostic tools for sex determination of the unborn. With social biases favouring the male child on consideration of economic advantages and the deep-rooted attitude of labelling the girl child as more of a liability, the sex ratio in the country has been highly skewed.

The process of elimination continues even after birth in various forms of discrimination in matters of health, nutritional and educational needs of the girl child. Therefore, it has been rightly stated that women's disempowerment begins even before birth.

Concomitantly, the fact remains that empowerment of women leads to all-round progress of the society and emancipation from backwardness of beliefs and unscientific practices. The new media and communication methods need to be utilised fully towards driving this message home among the rural folks who cling to superstitious beliefs and practices. The 'Beti Bachao, Beti Padhao' campaign has been launched to achieve this objective of bringing about the awareness and the change.

What Modi said

Lamenting that we have an 18th century mindset, the Prime Minister called for an end to the discrimination between sons and daughters. He said this is the key to ending female foeticide. Modi reminded the medical fraternity, which also contributed to female foeticide, that their medical education had been for the purpose of saving lives and not killing daughters.

The Prime Minister also launched the 'Sukanya Samriddhi Account' for the benefit of the girl child. He released a stamp on the theme of 'Beti Bachao, Beti Padhao' (BBBP) and administered the 'Beti Bachao, Beti Padhao' pledge on the occasion.

Today the society as a whole needs to change its attitude towards the girl child to end female foeticide. The practice is prevalent among every strata of the society. Although there is a healthy sex ratio in the north-eastern region and tribal areas, in many parts of the country the incidence of female foeticide is high.

The Government has initiated this innovative scheme to save the lot of girl children.

INDIA LAUNCHES CAMPAIGN TO SAVE, EDUCATE GIRLS

"We cannot be counted as citizens of the 21st century" Indian Prime Minister Narendra Modi said in a hard-hitting message to the country during the launch of a nationwide campaign to save and educate girls. Modi said the practice of aborting female fetuses is worse than an 18th century mindset because girls are being killed even before they are born.

The prime minister said placing sons above daughters is a psychological illness of the entire country, and he called for a social awakening to treat girls on par with boys.

Modi said no mother wants to get rid of her child, but family and social pressures make her complicit in this crime.

In traditional Indian culture, sons are looked upon as assets - breadwinners and caretakers of their parents in their old age. Girls are regarded as a liability because parents have to give a dowry when she marries. Studies show that since ultrasounds made sex determination possible, as many as 12 million girls may have been aborted during the past four decades in India.

Modi launched the campaign to "Save the Daughter, Teach the Daughter" in Panipat in the northern Haryana state, a prosperous region that has the lowest number of girls to boys in the country - 879 for 1,000 males. The national average is 917 girls for 1,000 males. The program is aimed at improving the child sex ratio and gender equality through education and will focus on 100 districts where the gender ratio is critical. Among a host of measures, it will enforce existing laws that ban female feticide and improve attendance of girls in schools.

Maneka Gandhi, Women and Child Development Minister, said the gender situation is dire in some states like Haryana. She said the situation is so bad that according to government estimates no girls have been born for many years in 70 villages. Gandhi added that in some villages there are only 500 girls for every 1,000 boys. Female feticide takes place across economic classes and urban and rural areas, even better off and more educated women living in cities often prefer sons.

Asking people where they would get daughters in law if girls are not born, the prime minister said that for every 1,000 boys, 1,000 girls should be born. He called for a commitment from all states, villages, and local councils in the country to join hands in this goal. A U.N. study last year warned the dwindling number of girls in the country has reached "emergency proportions" and is fueling an increase in crime such as kidnapping and trafficking of women.

BENEFITS OF 'BETI BACHAO BETI PADHAO' SCHEME

There's a powerful saying, "When you educate a man, you educate a man but when you educate a woman, you educate a generation". This is because of the benefits of educating girls permeates the entire family and have far-reaching impacts within the entire society.

Women make up for almost half of the total population of India but they still lag behind men in a lot of areas. It is harrowing to note that a lot of females are not even allowed to be born. Many of those who are fortunate enough to see this world are denied of some of their most basic rights: quality education and healthcare. Many are married off in their teenage. Over the last many years, a significant fraction of number of women has been at the receiving end of discrimination and exploitation. Needless to say, it should be government's top priority to empower women in a country like India that has witnessed male domination for years.

Women upliftment is nearly impossible if issues like illiteracy, inequality, sexual harassment and female infanticide are not combated in the right manner. The year 2015 saw the launch of a flagship scheme by the Government of India, 'Beti Bachao, Beti Padhao' (Save daughters, educate daughters). The scheme aims to beget awareness regarding the waning Child Sex Ratio (CSR), apart from perking up the efficiency of several welfare schemes that have been rolled-out for women. The programme is being administered through a well-framed national campaign and a focussed multi-sectorial effort in 100 districts having a shallow CSR.

As Census data lays down, in the year 2001 the child sex Ratio in India (0-6 years) was a mere 927 girls per 1,000 boys, which further declined in 2011 to a staggering 918 girls for every 1,000 boys.

To address this dwindling CSR is one of the core intentions of this scheme and it is garnering massive support from NGOs like Save the Children who are already doing pioneering work in fostering girl child education and welfare. NGOs work through the support of philanthropic individuals, many of whom donate online to contribute to the good of the society. 'Beti Bachao Beti Padhao' is a collaborative initiative being run by Ministry of Women and Child Development, Ministry of Human Resource Development and Ministry of Health and Family Welfare and it covers all Indian states and union territories. The scheme has three primary objectives:

Prevent female infanticide

The steep downfall in the CSR is a prime indicator of women disempowerment in the country. CSR puts a light on the pre-birth discrimination on the basis of gender that manifests in the form of unacceptable practice of female infanticide. Convergent efforts by government agencies and NGOs are crucial to ensure survival, safety and empowerment of the fairer sex.

Under the scheme, district authorities are required to effectively monitor and ensure that the use of sex-determination tools by families and doctors lead to stringent action by law. Several healthcare centres indulging in such practices have been sealed owing to this programme. Parents, families, doctors and the community at large are being oriented to not resort to sex-determination during pregnancy.

Devise new schemes and work cohesively to ensure that every girl child is secured and protected

BBBP programme is being implemented with full commitment of government officials across the country. These officials are working in close coordination with each other in order to ensure survival, well-being, security and education of the girl children. The government has been actively working to converge BBBP with other schemes that have been implemented for the well-being of girls in India. Several sub-schemes have also been rolled out as a part of the umbrella BBBP scheme. For instance, Sukanya Samriddhi scheme is a small savings scheme wherein the parents of a girl or a legal guardian can open a dedicated savings account for her in any post office or in some of the authorized commercial banks. One needs to make contribution to the scheme for the first 14 years only. In the remaining seven years one will earn interest from the scheme without depositing.

Ensure every girl child gets quality education

This is a very significant aspect of the BBBP scheme. Right to Education Act, 2010 entitles every child the right to free education till the completion of elementary education in a neighbourhood school. Unfortunately, the Act does not see its proper implementation in letter and spirit. If the girls are educated properly, they will grow up to be self-empowered individuals, better equipped to take their socio-economic decisions in their own and society's best interests. Under the BBBP scheme, district-level education officials have to ensure that the benefit of free elementary education reaches all the girls in their areas. There is active involvement of schools and other grass root- level organisations in this. The school management committees that are able to achieve 100% transition of girl students at various educational levels are awarded under the BBBP scheme.

EDUCATION IS A GIFT FOR LIFE

Education is a gift for life. We help children reach school and stay there. We help children unlock their potential and realize their dreams. We believe that every child is extraordinary and can scale great heights if provided with the right learning opportunities. With regular and generous contributions from our supporters, we are able to march steadily towards achieving these goals.

We are committed to ensure that all children, irrespective of their origin, are able to go to school, play, interact and learn with other children of their age. We help children with limited means hone their creativity and skills under the guidance of trained teachers and make persistent efforts to enable them to secure a life of dignity for themselves, their families and the community at large. In nine states of India, Save the Children runs programmes to support the education of the most disadvantaged children of India in different ways.

How do we do it?

We counsel parents from humble backgrounds to send their children to school and assist them through the admission process. In schools, we make learning fun. We train teachers to impart learning using child-friendly and interactive teaching-learning methods. We set libraries and infrastructure right, conduct computer and English classes, promote and facilitate extra-curricular activities and sports.

We work with the local communities to form Children Groups (CGs) and School Management Committees (SMCs) and work with them to ensure that they take accountability of the development of the children in their community and that even the most marginalized children in their area are sent to school and they stay there. We map out-of-school children and ensure their enrolment into formal schools in age-appropriate classes.

In classrooms, we encourage and help children to undertake learning activities in groups. This makes the entire experience much more fun and promotes healthy competition. In metro cities, we operate our own learning centres where children coming from the socially-excluded communities are provided learning and/or after-school support. For example, in Kolkata and Mumbai, we run Mobile Learning Centres which reach the doorsteps of the children who need us most.

During emergencies, we set up Temporary Learning Centres and distribute education kits so that that the affected children do not drift away from the path of education.

BECAUSE I AM A GIRL (CAMPAIGN)

Because I Am a Girl is an international campaign by the aid organization Plan. The campaign is made to address the issue of gender discrimination around the world. The goal of the campaign is to promote rights of girls and bring millions of girls out of poverty around the world. It is part of the organization's broader international development work. The campaign focuses on inequality faced by girls in developing countries, and promotes projects to improve opportunities for girls in education, medical care, family planning, legal rights, and other areas.

Campaign goals

Plan International states that the campaign has several current goals, which in 2012 included:

- Girls' education to be prioritised by world leaders
- Girls' completion of a quality secondary education to be a major focus of international action
- Funding for girls' education to be increased
- An end to child marriage
- An end to gender-based violence in and around schools
- Participation of girls and boys in decision making and inspiring those with power to take action

Plan has targeted 4 million girls through direct programs and projects, and has the goal of reaching 40 million girls and boys indirectly through gender programs. Plan has a further goal of positively impacting 400 million girls through lobbying for governmental policy changes.

Origins

The campaign began shortly after Plan International published its first annual report on the state of the world's girls in May 2007, titled "Because I am a Girl". The widely cited report, principally written by Nikki Van der Gaag, compiled and analyzed research into the extent of discrimination against girls worldwide and in the developing world in particular. Violence against girls, forced child marriage, endemic poverty, and many other topics were examined. Plan International developed the Because I am a Girl campaign as an ongoing initiative to launch projects aimed at remedying the challenges faced by girls.

Annual reports

Each year, a *Because I Am a Girl* report is released by Plan as an update on the state of the world's girls. The report has been produced annually since 2007. Researchers for the report visit girls throughout the world and summarize their findings in the report.

Reports released since 2007:

- 2007: The State of World's Girls
- 2008: In the Shadows of War
- 2009: Girls in the Global Economy: Adding It All Up

- 2010: Digital and Urban Frontiers
- 2011: Because I am a Girl: So What About the Boys?
- 2012: Because I am a Girl: Learning for Life
- 2013: In Double Jeopardy: Adolescent Girls and Disasters
- 2014: Pathways to Power: Creating Sustainable Change for Adolescent Girls
- 2015: The Unfinished Business of Girls' Rights

International activity

Plan International has raised awareness of its campaign through innovative marketing, including a highly visible bus stop poster campaign.

Plan International also initiated the International Day of the Girl Child, adopted by the United Nations General Assembly as an annual observance day. The inaugural International Day of the Girl Child was October 11, 2012.

Canada

Plan Canada's *Because I Am a Girl* initiative created a petition to the Canadian government for a National Day of the Girl. This petition was designed to lobby the United Nations for an International Day of the Girl, initially to be observed on September 22. The stated goal was to bring international attention and awareness on the issue of gender inequality and allow for girls to obtain their rights. Canada sponsored a resolution in the United Nations General Assembly to observe the International Day of the Girl Child each October 11, a resolution that the UN voted to adopt.

United Kingdom

In a 2009 campaign, celebrity women donated pictures from their childhood, discussed women who inspired them, and gave their thoughts on human rights.

In 2014, a school girl wrote a poem about forced marriage after discovering the Because I Am a Girl campaign. Her poem was published online by Plan UK.

United States

In 2015, Mo'ne Davis teamed up with the brand M4D3 (Make A Difference Everyday) to design a line of sneakers for girls, with some of the proceeds going toward the Plan International's Because I Am a Girl campaign.

Conclusion

The Beti Bachao Beti Padhao scheme is a praiseworthy initiative by the Government of India to address the issues revolving around girl children in India, right from the time they aren't even born to them turning adults. Apart from generating global headlines, the initiatives under the scheme have started bearing fruit as the level of awareness among the masses to work for girl child upliftment is increasing. An assessment of the scheme is due in July 2016. Success of this scheme will add tremendously to the economic growth of the nation. This is because to march ahead, India cannot afford having a large part of its population remain neglected and marginalised.

2

Beti Bachao, Beti Padhao Yojana

According to prime minister – Mr Narenda Modi : "Our Mantra should be: 'Beta Beti, Ek Samaan'" .

We have provided essay on Beti Bachao Beti Padhao, a scheme launched by the Prime Minister Narendra Modi, in order to help students as they generally get assigned in their schools for writing essay on the social schemes. All the Beti Bachao Beti Padhao essay are written using very simple words under various words limit according to the class standard of students. Essay or paragraph writing competitions have been very common in the schools in order to improve student's writing skill.

Beti Bachao Beti Padhao is a government social scheme launched by the Prime Minister Narendra Modi in order to address the gender imbalance and discrimination against girl child in the Indian society. This scheme was launched by the Prime Minister on 22nd of January in 2015 at Panipat, Haryana on Thursday. This scheme is to aware people about the importance of girls in the society. It is to increase awareness among common people to save the lives of girl child by completely removing the female foeticide. People should celebrate the birth of their girl child and educate them with full responsibility as they do for their boy child.

Beti Bachao Beti Padhao (means save the girl child and educate the girl child) is a scheme launched by the government of India in the month of January in 2015. The purpose of launching this scheme was generating awareness as well as improving the efficiency of welfare services for women and girl child in the

Indian society. The initial capital required for initiating this scheme was Rs 100 crore. The launch of this was very much required as according to census data of 2001, child sex ratio of age group 0-6 years was 927 girls/1000 boys in our country. It was seen a huge drop in the sex ratio 918 girls/1000 boys in 2011. India was ranked 41st among 195 countries worldwide by the UNICEF in 2012 that's why the scheme for girls was very necessary to aware people about the safety of women all over India. This scheme also make a call to people to eradicate female foeticide.

Beti Bachao Beti Padhao programme is a nationwide scheme launched purposefully to address the issue of decreasing girl child ratio in the society as well as empowering girl child in the country. This scheme was successfully launched by the Indian Prime Minister Narendra Modi on 22nd of January in 2015 at Panipat, Haryana. This scheme is to make people aware of the importance of girl child in the Indian society as well as bring some positive changes in the people mindset towards girl child. People in the Indian society have very rude mindset about the girl child. They think that girls are like burden in their life who only need to take whole life from their parents or husbands and never give.

However, it is not true, girls occupy almost half population of the world so they are half responsible for the existence of life on the earth. Less importance of girl child in the human society is causing suspense of life existence on the earth as where there is no women, no new birth would be. The continuous decrease in the ratio of girl child per boy child is clearing this issue very well. So, this scheme has been launched by keeping in mind to prevent sex determination, female foeticide, save girl child, ensure safety of girl child, as well as provide quality education to them.

Beti Bachao Beti Padhao scheme is a government scheme launched by the Prime Minister of India in the month of January in 2015. This programme was launched to make some positive changes in the Indian society in status of girl child. There are many restrictions for the girl child in the Indian society which hinders the proper growth and development of the girl child. This scheme hinders the practice of female foeticide, girl child insecurity, sex discrimination, etc against girl child. People's mindset for women has been more worse in the modern time than the people of 18th century".

While launching the programme prime minster said that, Indian people have common belief for girls that they are the property of someone else other than their parents. Parents think that only boys are their property as they have to look after them in the old age however girls have to go another place to care her in-laws.

Such thinking of people of 21st century about girls is really embarrassing and need to be eradicated from the people's mind for giving the full rights of girl child from birth. The condition of girl child was much worse in the last decades as female foeticide was getting practiced to a great extent. Girl children were killed in the mother's womb through proper detection techniques before birth.

This practice was in vogue to reduce the number of girl child as well as avoid the responsibility of a girl child. Haryana was chosen as the best place to launch the scheme as Mahendragarh district in Haryana has the worst sex ratios of girl child in the country (775 girls/1000 boys).

Beti Bachao Beti Padhao is a government scheme launched by the PM Narendra Modi on 22nd of January on Thursday, at Panipat, Haryana. This scheme has been launched by keeping in mind the drastic condition of girl child in the Indian society. According to the statistics, the ratio of girl child per male child (of age group 0-6 years) was 945/1000 in 1991 whereas it remains only 927/1000 in 2001 and again reduced to 918/1000 in 2011. If we see the census report we see that the ratio of girl child is decreasing continuously per each decade.

It is a danger sign related to the possibility of life on the earth. If nothing is applied positively on urgent basis to reduce such type of issues against girls, surely there would be a day without women and new births.

Keeping in mind this bad figure of girl child in the country, Prime Minister Narendra Modi has launched the scheme Beti Bachao Beti Padhao. It is a very effective scheme aims to improve the number of girl child, save girl child, eradicate female foeticide, give them proper security and education, personal and professional development, etc all over the country. This scheme has been implemented in 100 selected districts of the country (by the joint initiative of ministry of Human Resource Development and Health and ministry of Women and Child Development) through a national campaign in order to cover all the states and UTs.

There are some positive aspect that this scheme would be proved as a great start to remove social issues against girl child. We hope that there would be a day when no girl child would be killed, uneducated, insecure, raped, etc because of socio-economic reasons. Hence, Beti Bachao Beti Padhao scheme is aimed to make girls independent both socially and financially by reducing the sex discrimination all over the country.

Prime Minister Narendra Modi has launched a scheme for girls named Beti Bachao Beti Padhao in order to save the girl child and educate the girl child all over the India. The programme was launched on 22nd of January, Thursday in 2015 at Panipat,. This scheme was launched especially in Haryana as this state has lowest female sex ratio (775 girls/1000 boys) all over the country.

It has been effectively implemented in hundred districts across the country to improve the status of girls. 12 districts (Ambala, Kurukshetra, Rewari, Bhiwani, Mahendergarh, Sonepat, Jhajjar, Rohtak, Kaithal, Panipat, Karnal, and Yamuna Nagar) have been chosen from the Haryana state itself because of having low child sex ratio.

In order to improve the status of girls and give them importance, Haryana Government celebrates an event named Beti ki Lohri on January 14. The purpose of launching Beti Bachao Beti Padhao scheme is to make girls independent socially and financially using their proper rights and higher education. It helps in improving the awareness among common public and improving the efficiency of welfare services given to women. If we have a sight on latest census report of 2011, we see a continuous decrease in the female child sex ratio (of age group 0-6 years) from last some decades.

In 2001, it was 927/1000 whereas in 2011 it remains only 919/1000. There is huge reduction in the number of girls is because of the practice of aborting female fetus after sex determination through modern diagnostic tools in the hospitals. This bad practice came into existence because of the gender discrimination in the society.

And, after birth of a girl child, she has to face another type of discrimination in terms of education, health, nutrition, safety, rights, and other needs of the girl child. We can say that women were dis-empowered instead of being empowered. In order to empowering women and give them their full rights right from their birth government of India has launched this scheme. Empowering women brings all around progress especially in the family and society. Beti Bachao Beti Padhao scheme is the way to achieve positive changes in the human negative mindset for girls.

This scheme may make a call to people to end the discrimination between sons and daughters and work as a key to end female foeticide. While launching the scheme, PM reminded to the whole medical fraternity that the purpose of medical profession is to save lives and not finish lives.

Beti Bachao Beti Padhao (BBBP)

"save daughter, educate daughter" is a Scheme that fits its words means it aims to generate awareness among Indian Women and by saying this improve the efficiency of welfare services meant for women. BBBP Scheme was launched by the Prime Minister on 22nd January, 2015 at Panipat of Haryana State.

The scheme will have focused intervention and multi-section action in almost 100 districts with low Child Sex Ratio (CSR) So from 2015 women and girl child are going to be highly beneficial and an awareness and empowerment will increase among society specially women.

What is BBBP and Beti bacahao Beti Padhao) Scheme

Beti Bachao Beti Padhao Scheme addresses the declining Child Sex Ratio (CSR) and related issues of women empowerment over a life-cycle continuum.

It is a tri-ministerial effort of Ministries of India

- Women and Child Development
- Health & Family Welfare
- Human Resource Development.

According to census data, the child sex ratio ranging f(0–6 years) in India was 927 girls per 1,000 boys in 2001, which dropped drastically to 918 girls for every 1,000 boys in 2011. A 2012 UNICEF report ranked India 41st among 195 countries.

Objective and Primitives of Beti Bachao Beti Padhao Yojana

The Overall Goal of the Beti Bachao, Beti Padhao(BBBP) Scheme is to Celebrate the Girl Child & Enable her Education. This Yojana was launched under these objectives and perspectives.

Prevention of gender biased sex selective elimination

Today a large amount of female ratio is missing in ASIA . And india is top most country among this sex discrmination .So under this scheme it will be mainly focused the female male ratio and a huge step will be made towards prevention of Gender biased sex elimination.

Ensuring survival & protection of the girl child

Every day you see in news a lot of cases arise that a female foetus , an unborn female child was found dead wrapped in newspapers in dustbin, near railway station and in other areas. These happening make our country so sick and weak so Under Beti Bachao Beti Padhao Yojana it will the major step to ensure the survival and protection of each and Every Girl child that comes into focus .

Ensuring education and participation of the girl child

Saving the Girl child and securing will not help any how in making girls strong and making a better India , According to our prime minister Mr Narendra Modi ji – Every Girl in this country must be educated in order to make women achieve what they want.

Major Components Of Beti Bachao Beti Padhao Scheme

The Beti Bachao Beti Padhao (BBBP) initiative has two major components.

i) Mass Communication Campaign – The campaign aims at ensuring girls are born, nurtured and educated without discrimination to become empowered citizens of this country. The Campaign interlinks National, State and District level interventions with community level action in 100 districts, bringing together different stakeholders for accelerated impact.

ii) Multi-sectoral action in 100 selected districts (as a pilot) with adverse CSR, covering all States and UTs – Coordinated & convergent efforts are undertaken in close coordination with MoHFW and MoHRD to ensure survival, protection and education of the girl child. The District Collectors/Deputy Commissioners (DCs) lead and coordinate actions of all departments for implementation of BBBP at the District level. Mulit-sectoral interventions includes:

Ministry of WCD:

- Promote registration of pregnancies in first trimester in Anganwadi Centres (AWCs);
- Undertake training of stakeholders;
- Community mobilization & sensitization;
- Involvement of gender champions;
- Reward & recognition of institutions & frontline workers.

Ministry of Health & Family Welfare:

- Monitor implementation of Pre-Conception and Pre-Natal Diagnostic Techniques (PCP&DT) Act, 1994;
- Increased institutional deliveries;
- Registration of births;

- Strengthening PNDT Cells;
- Setting up Monitoring Committees

Ministry of Human Resource Development:

- Universal enrolment of girls;
- Decreased drop-out rate;
- Girl Child friendly standards in schools;
- Strict implementation of Right to Education (RTE);
- Construction of Functional Toilets for girls.

What can we all do as individuals:

- Celebrate the birth of girl child in the family and community
- Take pride in daughters and oppose the mentality of 'Bojh' and 'Paraya Dhan'.
- Find ways to promote equality between boys and girls.
- Secure admission to & retention of girl child in schools.
- Engage men and boys to challenge gender stereotypes and roles.
- Educate and sensitize our sons to respect women and girls as equal members of society.
- Report any incident of sex determination test.
- Strive to make neighborhood safe & violence-free for women & girls.
- Oppose dowry and child marriage within the family and community.
- Advocate simple weddings.
- Support women's right to own and inherit property.
- Encourage women to go out, pursue higher studies, work, do business, access public spaces freely etc.
- Mind his language and be sensitive to women and girls

How to apply for Beti Bachao Beti Padhao Yojana

Check the Following steps. The basic steps is first to open a bank account on the name of that girls child , but these are the following steps you must have to follow in order to get the benifits–

- Age limit for BBBP –According to this secheme the age limit for opening an account is upto 10Years, and there is buffer period of 1 Year. Means, the girl child who has attained the age of 10 years 1 year those are capable for this scheme. So final is that you can open BBBP account upto 11 years after the birth of Girl Child.
- Tax Free Scheme – This welfare scheme launched by prime minister is absolutely tax free means after opening BBBP account no amount will be deducted from your account wholewhile.
- Documents Required for Beti Bachao Beti Padhao Scheme – Make sure you must be having the following documents in order to open your account.
  1. Birth Certificate of Girl Child
  2. Identity proof of the parent or legal guardian
  3. Address proof of the parent or legal guardian

Note- NRI party is not applicable for this scheme.

As per RBI Guidelines, Rules and Regulations an NRI cannot apply for this scheme. The post office saving account rules, 1981, governs Sukanya Dev Yojna, so, NRIs doesn't come into this category.

- How much benifit Girl Child will Get – In BBBP Scheme Ministry of Women and Child Development is functioning in collaboration with Ministry of Health and Family Welfare as well as Ministry of Human Resource Development.

PM Mr. Modi called its a Boon and a enlightened step for the society. Also in this Yojana –

1. The Government also projected Rs 150 crore to be spent by the Ministry of Home Affairs on a scheme to extend the security of women in large cities of India .
2. The Union Budget has allocated to the Ministry of Road Transport and Highways Rs 50 crore for pilot schemes to safeguard the safety of women on public road transport.

Benifits of specially Girl Child are as follows –

1. Thorough this BBBP Yojana you will be opened your

daughter account , your girl child financial burden will be less and as you would get money for her small needs.

2. In BBBP scheme government offers the Highest Interest Rate among all Small Savings. So with this, you save more money for your daughter in future.
3. This BBBP account has been exempted. contribution to this account u/s 80C of the Income Tax Act, 1961. So your girl child account will be full of tax-free. Means no money will be deducted from that specified account as in terms of tax.
4. Best part of this Yojana is that – Maturity of account is 21 years from the date of opening of the account or Marriage of the Girl Child, through this account withdrawal is allowed on attaining the age of 18 years by girl child only if funds are required for Higher Education. The maximum period of this account is 21 years.
5. The main aim and Objective of of BBBP Yojana is To make people understand that girl child is not a burden for the parents for the girl education and for the marriage of girl through this account save money . It gives the complete financial security to the girl.
6. After completion of the account timing and girl age should be 21 years then all are the interest will be added in the girl account.

BETI BACHAO AWARENESS CAMPAIGN

Beti Bachao activities include large rallies, po campaigns, wall paintings, billboards, television commercials and short animations and video films. Celebrities such as video director Jagmeet Bal, and Bollywood actress Priyanka Chopra, have become involved in beti bachao beti padhao abhiyaan.

National support

The Beti Bachao campaign is supported by numerous medical organizations in India, including the Indian Medical Association.

Government support at the state level has provided funding for Beti Bachao publicity activities in particular. The expenditures

a "mental illness" Modi said that if this discrimination does not end it could cause a "terrible crisis" soon because of a lack of women in the country. Incidentally the PM launched the two schemes from Panipat in Haryana that has among the lowest child sex ratio in the country (837 girls to 1000 boys).

The launch was done amid much fanfare with senior Cabinet ministers Maneka Gandhi, Ravi Shankar Prasad, J P Nadda, Smriti Irani, Haryana CM M L Khattar and actor Madhuri Dixit present.

The PM who slammed the audience for "double standards" in killing daughters but desiring educated daughters-in-law also chose to attack doctors who assist in sex selective abortions.

In a speech that was met with much applause, he said, "We cannot call ourselves citizens of 21st century by practicing such a crime and we by our mindsets belong to 18th century when daughters were killed soon after they were born."

Pleading to end this ill practice, he said, "The Prime Minister of this country had come to them like a beggar and was begging for the lives of daughters."

Referring to Haryana, he said it was very painful for him to see that in a state which produced a woman like Kalpana Chawla, the first Indian woman to have travelled in space, "other Kalpana Chawlas are killed in the wombs of their mother".

He also launched Sukanya Samridhi Yojna (girl child prosperity scheme), under which girl children below 10 years will have bank accounts with more interest and income tax benefits.

The campaign will be initially implemented in the 100 districts, including 12 in Haryana, and across the country where the sex ratio is rather poor.

By persisting with such a discrimination against girl child, the nation would not only harm itself but also generations to come, the Prime Minister said, adding it will take a lot of commitment and many years before the imbalance in sex ratio ended.

Urging doctors to shun female foeticide, Modi said they were not given education for killing girl child and that it was their responsibility as part of society to ensure girls' safety and progress.

"I want to ask you if this is what you have to do to make money... This sin is a betrayal against society," he said.

Terming as a "myth" that sons take care of parents in their old age, Modi said had it been true, then so many old age homes would not have come up in the last 50 years. "There are countless number of families where parents are unhappy despite having sons and where parents are happy due to their daughter," he said.

Citing the incident in 2006 which a five-year-old boy Prince was rescued in an over 50-hour operation after he had fallen into a borewell in Kurukshetra, he said the whole country had prayed for him. He wondered why the same people become so insensitive when so many girl children are killed around them.

Stressing the need for quality education for girls, he said the fact that parents do not educate their daughters well but want well-educated daughters-in-law reflects society's "double-standard".

Women and child development minister Maneka Gandhi said the 'beti bachao, beti padhao' campaign was the fourth major initiative of the Modi government after Jandhan Yojna, Swachh Bharat Abhiyan and Make in India campaign. She added that 2000 girls are killed every day in the country which was "shameful."

A reward of Rs 1 crore will be given for the "innovative" village which attains a balanced sex ratio. Gandhi said there were 70 villages in the state where no girl child had been born for years.

3

Improving Girls' Education and Status in India with Beti Bachao, Beti Padhao

On July 17, a 6-year old girl was raped in an upscale private school in Bangalore, one of the premier cities of India. Reports of horrific sexual assaults and the very recent rapes and murders by hanging of two teen girls in Badaun still haunt Utter Pradesh. The statements issued by chief ministers in response to the rapes were also revealing of a general attitude of apathy and misplaced tolerance: "Boys will make mistakes." When it comes to girls and their safety, what is communicated is that there are more important issues to deal with and these situations should not garner so much attention. "Is there no other news?" the chief minister of Karnataka snapped at the reporter when he was asked to comment on the shocking rape of the 6 year old.

These cases of sexual violence and abuse are but a few instances of a deeper malaise known to afflict the entirety of India deeply.

In 2007, the Ministry of Women and Child Development, with the help of UNICEF, Save the Children and Delhi-based organization Prayas, reported that two out of three Indian children face physical abuse and more than half face sexual abuse in some form. Children in institutional care reported the highest incidence of sexual abuse and assault. The Asian Center for Human Rights found that child rapes had increased by 337 percent over 10 years, increasing from 2,113 incidences in 2001 to 7,112 in 2011.

India is also home to one-third of the 10 million child brides in the world. When girls are forced to marry at 14 years and younger, they are physically, economically and sexually bound to strangers they have never seen. They have no voice or say in the matter, no negotiating power, and no rights of refusal or choice in their sexual relations with their new husband. Is this not also the definition of rape? According to the United Nations Population Fund, more than two-thirds of married women between 15 and 49 years have been beaten and forced to provide sex. The law protecting children from sex abuse was only recently enacted in 2012 with criminal domestic violence laws only enacted in 2005.

Not only are women and girls unsafe at home, but their vulnerability extends to learning environments. India has 3.8 million girls still out of school, and unsafe and ill-equipped school environments are a further deterrent for parents to send their girls to school. According to India's 2011 census, 53 percent of households and 11 percent of schools had no toilets. This is a significant safety hazard for girls and women and gives them no other choice but to expose and relieve themselves in unsafe and public places. What is the government of India doing to address this problem?

The current administration has made some positive moves by announcing a Beti Bachao Beti Padhao campaign—the Save Daughters, Educate Daughters campaign. Coupling girls' safety and their education is both insightful and intelligent, provided there is a deeper realization of what this entails. The interim budget has allocated 100 crore rupees (1 billion rupees) specifically for this campaign, and another 50 crore rupees will go toward women's safety in public transport and 150 crore rupees toward women's safety in large cities.

Though the intentions are laudable, it has been pointed out by some that while 1 billion rupees have been allocated to women's safety, twice that amount was allocated to the construction of a statue for Sardar Patel, a statesman and freedom fighter. This contrast speaks volumes of the actual importance given to girls and women by the government.

While girls' education has received some attention as a result of global advocacy, a wider view of education is needed and should undoubtedly include the physical, social and political circumstances in which girls are living. Several steps need to be taken in order to give concrete shape to the Beti Bachao Beti Padhao campaign and educators in India have an important role to play.

First, education should include gender studies in the core curriculum of schools so that students examine gendered social norms critically and learn to develop egalitarian constructions of masculinity and femininity. Boys and young men must be educated in schools to value and respect women and girls, take responsibility for the increasing violence against girls, and respect girls' rights to their own bodies. Girls must be empowered by their education to speak up when they are abused, protest unwanted advances and protect themselves, and to demand their right to bodily integrity and respect in and outside of their homes. Educators must address communities and teach them to value their daughters for more than the sexual, domestic and reproductive labor they provide.

Next, immediate action must be taken to provide the infrastructure required to ensure the safety of girls and women on the streets, in schools and other institutions. This means adequate and separate toilets in schools and elsewhere. To his credit, Prime Minister Narendra Modi addressed the issue of women's safety specifically in his address to the Nation on August 15th, India's Independence day. He urged parents to focus on the upbringing of their sons, promised separate toilets for girls in all schools, and urged big corporations to direct their social responsibility funds to this end. Within a week two large corporations, Tata Consultancy Services and Bharti Enterprises, responded with contributions of 1 billion rupees each.

Lastly, civil society must keep up the pressure on the government so that crimes against girls and women are taken seriously. The police, judiciary and administration must take stern and expeditious actions when girls are violated anywhere—at home, in school, or on the streets. In addition to improved policing of these situations from law enforcement in general, increasing the number of women as police officers, bus drivers, and civil servants would also make a difference in ensuring equitable treatment is provided for many generations of girls to come.

PROCESS OF SAVE THE GIRL CHILD

India is growing dynamically in every fields. Today, the boom in economy, innovative technologies and improved infrastructure has become nation's pride. The country has witnessed advancements in all fields but bias against a girl child is still prevailing in the country. This social evil is deep rooted in Indian ethos and the most shocking fact is that the innovative and hard high end technologies are brutally killing the Indian girl child. Innovative techniques, like biopsy, ultrasound, scan tests and amniocentesis, devised to detect genetic abnormalities, are highly misused by number of families to detect gender of the unborn child. These clinical tests are highly contributing to the rise in genocide of the unborn girl child.

In today's day and age most couples prefer the process known as a planned pregnancy, because of various factors; prime amongst them being the financial well being to support the birth and nurturing of a child. In such cases, the first prenatal visit actually happens prior to actual pregnancy, to see whether one is ready to go off the contraception pills and conceive a baby. However, in maximum conceptions, one is unaware of the pregnancy until actual realization dawns after one skips the first menstrual cycle. Normally doctors except ladies to pay their first visit anywhere between the sixth and twelfth week after conception.

Amniocentesis started in India in 1974 to detect fetal abnormalities. These tests were used to detect gender for the first time in 1979 in Amritsar, Punjab. Later the test was stopped by the Indian Council of Medical Research but it was too late. The benefits of these tests were leaked out and people started using it as an instrument for killing an innocent and unborn girl child. Many of the traditional women organizations also took up cudgels to stop this illegal practice but all failed and with the passage of time these tests became a major contributor to bias against a girl child. Female feticide and infanticide is not the only issues with a girl child in India. At every stage of life she is discriminated and neglected for basic nutrition, education and living standard. When she was in the womb, she was forced to miss the moment when she was supposed to enter the world. At the time of birth her relatives pulled her back and wrung her neck. After killing her she was thrown into a trash can.

During childhood, her brother was loaded with new shoes, dresses and books to learn while she was gifted a broom, a wiper and lots of tears. In her teenage, she missed tasty delicious food to eat and got only the crumbs. During her college days, she was forced to get married, a stage where illiteracy, lack of education resulted in high fertility rate, aggravating the condition of females in the country. Again if this female gives birth to a girl child, the journey begins once again. She missed all roses of life and was finally fitted to a graveyard. That's where she got peace of mind.

The nation of mothers still follows a culture where people idolizes son and mourns daughters. UN figures out that about 750,000 girls are aborted every year in India. Abortion rates are increasing in almost 80% of the India states, mainly Punjab and Haryana. These two states have the highest number of abortions every year. If the practice continues, then no longer a day will come when Mother India will have no mothers, potentially, no life. We all are proud citizens of India. The need of hour is to realize our responsibilities and give a halt to this evil crime. What can we do to curb the brutal and undesirable practice of mass killing girls? A determined drive can initiate a spark to light the lamp and show the world that we all are part of the great Mother India..

THE EVOLUTION OF CHILDHOOD

Historically, the routine use of children as poison containers to prevent adults from feeling overwhelmed by their anxieties has also been universal. Examples from the history of childhood regularly reveal children are expected to "absorb" the bad feelings of their caretakers. As one peasant community in rural Greece puts it, you must have children around to put your bad feelings into, especially when the "Bad Hour" comes around. An informant describes the process as follows: One of the ways for the Bad Hour to occur is when you get angry. When you're angry a demon gets inside of you. Only if a pure individual passes by, like a child for instance, will the "bad" leave you, for it will fall on the unpolluted.

Newborn infants, in particular, were perfect poison containers because they were so "unpolluted." The newborn then became so full of the parent's projections that even if he or she is allowed to live (up to half the children in early societies were murdered at birth), the infant had to be tied up--tightly swaddled in bandages for up to a year or more---to prevent it from "tearing its ears off, scratching its eyes out, breaking its legs, or touching its genitals," i.e., to prevent it from acting out the violent and sexual projections of the parents.

Children were particularly useful as poison containers when adults felt anxious about recent or impending success. Success stirs up superego retaliation, and the sacrifice of children to appease the gods--that is, the punitive parents--was an extremely widespread guilt-reducing device. Most early states practiced child sacrifice. Typical was Carthage, where a large cemetery has been discovered called The Tophet filled with over 20,000 urns deposited there between 400 and 200 B.C. The urns contained bones of children sacrificed by their parents, who often would make a vow to kill their next child if the gods would grant them a favor--for instance, if their shipment of goods were to arrive safely in a foreign port. Some urns contain the bones of stillborn babies along with the bones of two-year-olds, indicating that if the promised child was not born alive, an older child had also to be killed to satisfy the promise.

The sacrifice was accompanied by a music, wild dancing and riotous orgy, and was probably accompanied by the ritual rape of virgin girls, as it was with the Incans. Plutarch told how the priests would "cut their throats as if they were so many lambs or young birds; meanwhile the mother stood by without a tear or moan [while] the whole area before the statue was filled with a loud noise of flutes and drums..." Sacrifice, rape and genital mutilation of young girls continues to take place today in the Andean mountains, particularly to ward off the guilt coming after successful cocaine deliveries. These ceremonies, from antiquity to today, resemble closely the satanic rituals made familiar recently in the newspapers, using the infliction of rape, sexual mutilation and other horrors in order to visit upon child victims elements of the traumas of the satanists' own childhood.

That child sacrifice was carried out mainly by the rich in each of these early societies confirms my theory that it is a guilt-reducing technique. Whenever new ventures were begun, children would be sacrificed. Whenever a new building or bridge was built, a child would be buried within it as a "foundation sacrifice." Children still play at capturing a child and making it part of the bridge in "London Bridge's Falling Down." Children's bodies were particularly useful in curing disease. Whatever one's physical ills, a child could be used to "absorb" the poison that was responsible. When, for instance, one wanted to be cured of leprosy, one was supposed to kill a child and wash one's body in its blood.

When one wanted to find out if a house whose previous occupants had died of plague was still infected or not, one rented some children to live in it for several weeks to see if they died--rather like the use of canaries in mines to detect poisonous gas. When one was impotent, depressed or had venereal disease, doctors prescribed having intercourse with a child. As late as the end of the nineteenth century, men who were brought into Old Bailey for having raped young girls were let go because "they believed that they were curing themselves of venereal disease."

Raping virgins was particularly effective for impotence and depression; as one medical book put it, "Breaking a maiden's seal is one of the best antidotes for one's ills. Cudgeling her unceasingly, until she swoons away, is a might remedy for man's depression. It cures all impotence." And, of course, whenever a parent had a disease, they always had their children handy to absorb the poison. Thus British doctors in the nineteenth century regularly found when visiting men who had venereal disease that their children also had the same disease--on their mouths, anuses or genitals.

No matter what anxieties one had, one had children always at hand to use to relieve them. The evolution of childhood from incest to love and from abuse to empathy has been a slow, uneven path, but one whose progressive direction is, I think, unmistakable. This evolution of parent-child relations is, I contend, an independent source of historical change, lying in the ability of successive generations of parents to live through their own childhood traumas a second time and work through their anxieties in a slightly better manner this second time around. It is in this sense that I say that history is like psychotherapy, which also heals through revisiting one's childhood traumas and reworking earlier anxieties. If the parent--the mother, for most of history--is given even the most minimal support by society, the evolution of childhood progresses, new variations in historical personality are formed, and history begins to move in new, innovative directions. The crucial relationship in this evolution is the mother-daughter relationship.

If little girls are treated particularly badly, they grow up to be mothers who cannot rework their traumas, and history is frozen. For instance, although China was ahead of the West in most ways during the pre-Christian era, it became "frozen" and fell far behind the West in evolutionary social and technological change after it adopted the practice of footbinding girls.

Similarly, the cliterodectomy of girls in Moslem societies has inhibited their social development for centuries, since it likewise puts a brake on the ability of the next generation of mothers to make progress in caring for their children.

Clearly, different groups have moved different distances up the ladder of psychological evolution, since some contemporary groups still practice brain-eating as our Paleolithic ancestors did, and different subgroups of our more advanced nations still terrorize and abuse their children in ways identical to those that were commonplace centuries ago, producing the "historical fossils" (early "psychoclasses") we now call borderline personalities and other severe character disorders. Your neighbor is as likely to be a result of medieval parenting as of modern parenting, so modern societies contain a full range of childrearing modes and psychoclasses.

The "generational pressure" for psychological change is not only an independent historical force--originating in inborn adult-child striving for relationship--it occurs independent of social and technological change, and can be found even in periods of economic stagnation. My "psychogenic theory of history" posits that a society's childrearing practices are not just one item in a list of cultural traits, but--because all other traits must be passed down from generation to generation through the narrow funnel of childhood--instead makes childrearing the very basis for the transmission and development of all other cultural traits, placing definite limits on what can be achieved in the material spheres of history.

The main source of childhood evolution is, I believe, the process I call psychogenesis, by which parents--mainly the mother for most of history--revisit a second time around the stages of childhood and undo to some extent the traumas they themselves endured. It is in this sense that history is like a psychotherapy of the generations, undoing trauma and giving historical personality a chance at a new start with every baby born. Only humans have brain networks that allow this miracle to take place. All cultural changes in the past 100,000 years of Homo sapiens sapiens are epigenetic, not genetic.

Regardless of changes in the environment, it is only when changes in childhood occur that epigenetic changes in the brain can occur and societies can begin to progress and move in unpredictable new directions that are more adaptive. That more individuated and loving individuals are ultimately more adaptive is understandable--because they are less under the pressures of infantile traumas and are therefore more rational in reaching their goals. But that this childhood evolution--and therefore all social evolution--is terribly uneven is also understandable, given the varying conditions under which parents all over the world have to conduct their childrearing tasks.

ACTION FOR GIRLS' EDUCATION

Nearly two-thirds of children who are denied their right to education are female. At the World Education Forum, Dakar, 2000, countries agreed on ensuring that by 2015 all children, particularly girls, will have access to complete free and compulsory education of good quality. As we approach 2012, what is the status of girls' education in India?

A focus on girls' education was put in place since the 1986 National Policy on Education and the 1992 Programme of Action, followed by the SSA programme launched in 2001, National Curriculum Framework in 2005 and the National Curriculum Framework for Teacher Education in 2010. These policies were complemented by other schemes such as National Programme for the Education of Girls at the Elementary Level, Kasturba Gandhi Balika Vidyalaya Scheme, both ensuring inclusion and quality education for girls. The Mahila Samakhya programme was launched in 10 states targeting marginalised sections of rural women. Access to education was also facilitated by separate schools for girls, availability of open learning resources, residential schooling, coaching facilities; scholarships, textbooks, uniforms and transport including bicycles. The Right of Children to Free and Compulsory Education (known as RTE) Act, 2010, charted a new roadmap for gender equality in education in India.

Delivery Mechanism

Despite all these efforts, surprisingly , a large number of girls still remain outside the education system . According to Karin Hulshof, Unicef India representative, out of 81% girls joining school at the primary level, around 50% drop out at the secondary level because of factors such as child marriage, child labour, etc. "We must not look at girls as a liability but as an asset. The Sarva Shiksha Abhiyan (SSA) and Right to Education (RTE) Act are tools that can empower the girl child. We need an effective delivery mechanism and have more gender-friendly classrooms," she said.

R Govinda, vice-chancellor , National University of Educational Planning and Administration (NUEPA), feels that though there are various policies in place, when it comes to implementation, there is a wide gap. "Through various policies we have placed the education of the girl child in the foreground. I feel, policywise , we are on the right track. The RTE has made education a fundamental right. After 25 years of prioritising girls' education, we have seen a tremendous change. But a lot more needs to be done."

He further adds, "We can address the problem by engaging at different levels. By getting all girls in school, by examining what happens in school by paying attention to the socio-emotional conditions of the girl child, what the child learns in class in terms of the quality, by providing trained female teachers and keeping a track of what happens to girls beyond schools. That is when the expectations of parents and the community come into effect."

National Vision

The United Nations Children's Fund (Unicef) and ministry for human resources development (MHRD) drafted a 'National vision for Girls' Education in India - Roadmap to 2015' with an aim to building a comprehensive approach towards girls' education, which was discussed at a twoday national convention in the Capital recently.

The Vision Document provides a framework for action for girls' education in India. The plan of action for the next one year is the Shiksha Ka Haq Abhiyan which will be the cornerstone for the implementation of RTE. The government will engage with the community , media, states, and other stakeholders to create an environment and mechanism to ensure implementation at every level for girls' education.

Key Recommendations

Implement strong legislation outlawing child labour, genderbased violence, and harassment of girls Provide residential facilities, transport and other incentives to attract qualified female teachers to particularly rural and remote schools Address safety issues of girls Gender-friendly classrooms and separate toilets.

EDUCATING A GIRL CHILD MEANS EDUCATING THE FAMILY

" I ask you all so earnestly to open girl's schools in every village and try to uplift them. If the Conditions of women are raised, then their children will, by their noble actions, glorify the name of the Country. " —Swami Vivekananda Today's girl child will be the mother of tomorrow. As a mother she can give her child a sound nursing and capable upbringing. A woman has the maximum impact on the social, economical decisions making in the family generally. At micro level, educated woman help in making the whole family including the older family members, understand the values and importance of education, and at macro level, educated women add to the social and economical development of the nation.

Girls education is like sowing the seed which gives rise to green, cheerful and full grown family plant. In ancient time girl's education had a significant place in the society. Gargi and Maitreyi played very encouraging role in spreading the education to a great extent. Women's social conditions started deteriorating with the passage of time. Instead of giving them education, they are being subjected to sufferings under Purdah System, Child marriage. In some states female infanticide is prevalent even today. A new culture of elimination of female foetus has gradually become rampant discrimination between the education of girl and boy is common in rural areas. Parents feel that the education of girls is a wastage as they will go to their husbands after marriage and more dowry have to be paid for a more educated girl. The poverty and illiteracy among the people is also big reason for not sending the girls to schools and colleges. But things are being changed, though slowly, but gradually.

The various awakening programmes launched by the government for encouraging the girls education, the introduction of TV's in rural areas, the 33% reservation given to females in Panchayats, have played positive role in this direction. Now the important of educating the girls is being felt. Several other policies, like 30% reservation to women candidates in services, enhanced subsidy to girls entrepreneurs, various self employment schemes launched for the benefits of women like Women Entrepreneur Development Programme, Self Help Groups of women have resulted in mobilizing and directing the parents to get their daughters educated. The educated women can help in eradicating many social evils prevalent in the society, like Dowry, killing the female foetus, discrimination in the matter of education of the girls , illiteracy and so on. Many programmes of the government like population control, polio eradication, programmes relating to the development of the rural area in which the cooperation and coordination of the rural masses are necessary, can well be taken care by the women representatives of the Panchayats. If these representatives are educated the implementation of the programs will be a grand success. Education gives effectiveness and confidence to the women.

Undoubtedly true that girl's education stimulates educational consciousness and civic sense among the family members. She can teach the family members more comfortably than anyone else. Illiteracy is the cause of many ills. The present day corruption in the bureaucracy particularly in the implementation of the schemes for the development of the rural segment to a large extent is because of the ignorance and illiteracy among the rural representatives. A woman influences the activities and decisions of family than anyone else. The educated girl can shoulder any kind of responsibility. See the example of Kalpana Chawla, Kiran Bedi, Sonia Gandhi, Sushma Swaraj, Uma Bharati, and so .. , everyone has earned a name in the society in our country. For the success of a person whether man or woman, education plays an important role. Education for the girls is more important as she not only builds the home but all routine responsibilities are taken care of by her. An educated woman not only helps in nourishing the family in a better way but can also help in earning. Rightly said that God made the mother because He could not be present every where. "One could judge the degree of civilization of a country by the social and political position of its women" -Charles Fourier

Education for a girl child means making the next generation well educated, full of virtues, free from the useless superstitions, confident and capable to do something good for the family, for the society and for the country as a whole. The present day girl is the mother of tomorrow. "Give me good mothers and I will give you a great nation" -Napoleon

She is the most crucial and reverend entity. She must be given all the necessary education. Ignoring her, keeping her illiterate means we are creating an illiterate and ignorant generation. So it is perfectly true that educating a girl child means educating a family.Development cannot be accelerated unless girls are given right education in right direction. Swami Vivekananda has rightly said, "Educate your women first and leave them to themselves, then they will tell you what reforms are needed."

MISSIONARIES AND GIRLS' EDUCATION

An increasing number of male missionaries arrived after 1813, often accompanied by wives or sisters who started classes for girls. They belonged to Protestant organizations like the Church Missionary Society (CMS), London Missionary Society (LMS), Scottish Presbyterian Mission (SPM), the Wesleyan Mission, and the American Madura Mission. Later female missionaries arrived on their own, enthusiastic about their work as teachers, nurses, and doctors for Indian women. Early girls' classes were begun in south India by Mrs. Bailey at Kottayam, Travancore (1816); Mrs. Rhenius at Palayamkottai, Tirunelveli (1823); Mrs. Drew at Vepery, Madras (1832); Mrs. Eckard in Madurai (1835).

They provided a network for Indian Christian women whom they trained as "suitable wives for pastors and teachers." Spinster Mary Anne Cooke began an early Protestant girls' school in Bengal in 1821, and then set up 30 others. At the age of 12, a Bengali woman convert named Hannah Catherine Mullens (1826–61) taught girls at Bhawanipore Mission School, left this to write Christian literature, and possibly married a British missionary. Mission curriculum consisted of reading, writing, arithmetic, Gospel teachings, sewing, and knitting, the last being taught even in tropical south India.

Western women missionaries braved poverty, intense heat, and other adversities to teach Indian women, and their work with low castes raised their literary rates. Seeing low-caste girls as victims of brahmans, they attempted to convert them with such vigour that the high castes kept their own daughters away. As the poor were drawn to mission schools through gifts of rice and other benefits, especially during famines, they were often called "rice Christians." However, most Hindu and Muslim girls at mission schools did not embrace Christianity. Knowing the role of women in transmitting traditions at home, they feared that cultural identity could be lost through conversion. Missionaries also knew this and thus relied on "Bible women" converts to preach to the family, and village women.

EDUCATIONAL DEVELOPMENT OF GIRLS AND WOMEN

Education has been regarded as the most significant instrument for changing women's subjugated position in the society. It not only develops the personality and rationality of individuals, but qualifies them to fulfil certain economic, political and cultural functions and thereby improves their socio-economic status. One of the direct expectations from educational development in a society is the reduction in the inequality among individuals and that is why Education was included as the basic right of every human being in the Universal Declaration of Human Rights. The constitution of UNESCO also directs its efforts to achieve 'The ideal of equality of educational opportunity without regard to race, sex or any distinction, economic or social'.

In India, the increase in the educational facilities and opportunities for women and the removal of traditional bars on entry of women to particular branches and levels of education, came to be supported by all champions of women's emancipation from the 19th Century onwards. However, the Indian reformers of the 19th Century wanted to educate women to perform their role as good wives and mothers and not to make them as direct active participants in the process of national development of the country. The colonial authorities generally supported this limited view-point of women's education. The expansion of education and health services in the 20th Century, however, precipitated a need for women teachers and doctors which resulted in the incorporation of these two vocations in the programme of women's education.

After independence, the Constitutional guarantee of equality changed the conceptual thinking of educational development of women and gave a call to women to play multiple roles in the polity, the economy and the society and the educational development of women began in that broad direction. This is amply evident in the Government's policy, reports of various committees and commissions set up for this purpose and in the objectives of Development Plans formulated after Independence. The National Policy of Education provides that "The Education of girls should receive emphasis not only on grounds of social justice but also because it accelerates social transformation". The very First Five Year Plan of Education stated "The general purpose and objective of Women's education cannot, of course, be different from the purpose and objectives of the men's edu- cation .... At the Secondary and even at the University stage women's education should have a vocational or occupational bias". Similarly, the Secondary Education Commission (1953) —ated that "In a democratic society where all citizens have to discharge their civic and social obligations, differences which may lead to variations in the standard of intellectual develop- ment achieved by boys and girls can be envisaged". The Re- port of the Committee on Differentiation of Curricula for boys and girls (1959) also emphasised on the same type of education and same role of men and women in the society. The Educa- tion Commission (1964-66) endorsed the recommendations of all committees and commissions about the equality in the edu- cational development of women. The Government's national policy also laid down that "The education system must produce young men and women of character and ability committed to national services and development. Only then will education be able to play its vital role in promoting national progress, creating a sense of common citizenship and culture and strengthening national integration".

In spite of the constitutional provision of equality and the recommendations of the committees and commissions about the provision for the same type of education for women as for men, the traditional limited view point of women's education, with a separate role of women in the society. has had a great influence on the planning for women's education. Before, however, we review the accelerated growth and progress of women's education and analyse the problems of their future development after independence, it will be interesting and informative to trace very briefly the history of women's education during British regime.

This historical background will be helpful in properly understanding the trends that have followed the achievements in the era after independence in this field.

WOMEN'S GENERAL EDUCATION AND LITERACY

- "As it is often said, knowledge to the poor is power to the poor. It is this that empowers the rural poor in VAWA projects."

Women's general education and literacy are important if they are to reach their full potential and become empowered. Illiteracy creates a situation of dependency on others that can limit an individual's prospects for empowerment. Many MFIs have found illiteracy to be a major stumbling block for their clients.

Some, like WEDTF, try to adapt by making sure that there is at least one literate member in every group or that at least one member has a literate child who can assist the group. Many MFIs use participatory training techniques that do not require literacy to educate clients, but very few are able to offer literacy training since most methods for providing it are relatively expensive and time-intensive for both staff and clients.

Although many illiterate entrepreneurs are able to keep accounts in their heads, their ability to interact with the formal sector will always be limited. Some NGOs such as World Education and Women's Empowerment Project in Nepal have come up with innovative and low-cost methods of training women in literacy that have significantly enhanced the empowerment benefits of the savings and credit groups to which the women belong.

By using existing lending groups and providing materials for women to train themselves, the literacy programmes have grown rapidly for a relatively low cost in contrast to many literacy initiatives. These programmes have shown that literacy and education contribute powerfully to empowerment and complement the financial independence that microfinance provides.

In the case of WEP, the literacy rate among its members rose from 21 per cent to 85 per cent during the first 30 months of the programme. Helen Sherpa of World Education writes, "In new groups these women start as 'nobodies' leading groups that have no money and no respect. These groups' funds grow and they become increasingly self-reliant breaking the hold of male money lenders and male family members over economic decisions.

This suddenly elevates the status of the groups as well as the individual members and leaders. Leaders in the groups become role models because these are 'women like them'—poorer women, women who have become literate later in life."

In addition, educating women has additional benefits for their children. World Education has documented that women who attend education programmes dramatically increase their commitment to educating their children and to educating their daughters in particular. Because lack of money for school fees is the major cause of school dropouts in Nepal as well as in many other countries, the income generated from microenterprises plays an important role in helping women realise their dreams for their children.

Kashf in Pakistan found a similar linkage. An independent study found that 35 per cent of Kashf members see their educated loan officers as role models for their daughters. More than 50 per cent of the women wanted to educate their daughters, and more than 40 per cent wanted to pursue a different future for them.

Balancing Family and Work Responsibilities

In addition to educational disadvantages, one of the most difficult challenges that many women face as they start or expand businesses is the balancing of their increasing business responsibilities with their household responsibilities. Although the ultimate goal may be for household responsibilities to be shared between the men and women in the household, this sharing never happens overnight.

In many cases, women's businesses remain small and concentrated in less profitable sectors in large part because of the time constraints that women's domestic responsibilities create. Not only do women have limited time to spend on their business activities, but often they also must be able to abandon them altogether for periods to deal with family crises or children's illnesses.

As a result, many women's employment opportunities are limited to those that can be done on a part-time and often irregular basis. The experiences of Opportunity International's partners have demonstrated that women often need help to develop strategies for managing and meeting the expectations of family and community members while still having the time and energy to run their businesses well. Women also need support in negotiating the complex changes in gender roles that must ultimately take place in order for them to succeed as microentrepreneurs.

Many of Sinapi Aba Trust's clients as well as clients of Opportunity International's other partners in Africa have highly valued the advice on time management and "managing your husband" that they have received. Some Opportunity partners and other MFIs are also recognizing that more outreach efforts are necessary to secure husbands' cooperation and support.

It comes as no surprise that the most successful clients of many MFIs are the ones who have the most supportive husbands and that those with more problems often have problems with their husbands as well. Because most MFIs deal primarily with women, however, husbands are often not directly included.

Some MFIs are experimenting with ways to influence husbands through including them in selected orientation sessions, having special events for spouses, and inviting them to group meetings occasionally.

Dialogue on Social and Political Issues

Discussion of social issues affecting women's lives and communities can lead to greater awareness of the causes of the problems they face and allow them to take more effective action to address the problems that are holding them back. Discussion of women's rights, community problems, politics, and common family problems can foster a sense of solidarity that can empower women both as individuals and as a group to address their problems.

With some support, groups of economically empowered women can take steps to address the cultural and legal barriers that limit their social and political empowerment. CSD, for example, found that as a result of the discussions of social and legal issues held in lending centers, women have greater knowledge of their civil and legal rights and are more aware of their position and the choices they can make.

They have increased knowledge of how relevant institutions can help them when they need legal assistance, and this knowledge has allowed more women to resist domestic violence and alcoholism and demand fair minimum wages. Several studies point to the importance of social and cultural structures in determining an individual's level of empowerment or social value.

For example, a study by Dreze and Sen shows us that "structural variables making up gender relations in different parts of India are far more important in determining the extent to which the girl child is valued within the family than the individual characteristics of their parents."

Other studies show that structural characteristics are more important in determining the social value or empowerment of an individual than any of the individual's actions or circumstances are—including participation in microenterprise programmes.

These findings underscore the importance of at least attempting to address some of the wider social structures that are contributing to the disempowerment of women as well as helping women tackle some of the personal problems that are limiting their potential.

More formal training programmes on topics such as women's rights, domestic violence prevention, and family planning could substantially improve women's ability to face these challenges. Such education efforts, however, will likely be most successful when they are developed in cooperation with the clients themselves.

At SAT, Trust Banks develop their own education and training programmes in each loan cycle in cooperation with their loan officers. This ensures that the training provided and the topics discussed are those most relevant and useful to the clients. In many Grameen replications, the women control their own programme through their centers.

Such training and discussion does not have to be expensive to provide, and the potential benefits of empower-ment far outweigh the costs. Involving the women themselves in planning and even preparing training can help keep costs low while at the same time giving women the power to control their programme.

Experience in Decision Making and Leadership

One of the positive contributions that group-based lending methodologies make to women's empowerment is the opportunity for women to gain experience in making decisions and leading and influencing others. As Essma Ben Hamida of ENDA Interarabe in Tunisia puts it, "Participation in the micro-credit programme constitutes an apprenticeship of democracy through the self-managed solidarity groups which elect their president and treasurer: in many mixed groups, a woman has been elected as president, an astounding development in a still male-dominated society."

When they join microfinance programmes, many women have had little opportunity to voice their opinions or participate in decision making. Some will have had little experience even formulating an opinion that can be expressed since they have had little opportunity to do so.

A synthesis study done by Jennefer Sebstad and Monique Cohen found that "[lending] groups provide a means for women to know and be known by other women; a forum for learning leadership and public speaking skills; and a basis for development of trust, friendship, and financial assistance."

Although actual levels of control vary according to methodology, in most cases, women are called upon to develop and use skills in group dynamics and persuasion, to exercise authority, and to command the respect of others—some for the first time in their lives.

Opportunities for leadership are affected not only by the structure of the programme but also by the group's internal policy. Groups that set policies to rotate their leadership frequently give more women a chance to develop leadership skills than ones that do not, although groups without a rotation policy can allow a few women to develop even stronger and more lasting leadership skills. In addition, if the rotation of leadership is coupled with specific training on leadership and organizational skills, it can help foster a sense of equality among the women and break down other social barriers such as caste as well as gender. Programmes like SAT's deliberately try to break down traditional notions of leaders being chosen from an elite in order to instill the idea that everyone is capable of being a leader.

Mixed-sex and mixed-caste lending groups have the potential to empower, but if such groups do not make a deliberate effort to stimulate the meaningful participation of all members, they may end up replicating existing patterns of social inequality.

Much depends on the policies established, however, and some trade-offs in empowerment may apply, because allowing groups complete freedom to establish their own policies incurs a greater risk of replicating existing social structures and putting the same people in power inside the lending group as outside. In contrast, setting guidelines for internal policies can help promote healthy leadership experiences but constrains the autonomy of the groups.

MFIs can help maximize the empowerment potential of lending groups by providing training and coaching to client leaders, developing cost-effective methods for clients to manage their own loans and savings, ensuring that women have a chance to lead in mixed lending groups, and encouraging the active participation of all group members.

4

Female Foeticide and Gender Discrimination

Despite being proud of a legacy of strong queens and women leaders, girl children are not safe in the country. That is, if they are born at all. Female foeticide and gender discrimination are rampant, so much so that the sex ratio in many states is skewed and calamitous.

According to news reports, the sex ratio in India as of 2014 is 943 females to 1000 males. Some states are well below this national average – Haryana has a sex ratio of 879 females to 1000 males. An allied evil is discrimination based on the child's gender. Girl children in India are often denied education and healthy nutrition too. Prime Minister Narendra Modi's 'Beti Bachao-Beti Padhao' campaign is one giant step in generating awareness and combating this evil, and yet India has to make much progress in this area. Female foeticides are surprisingly, much higher in number in urban India than in rural areas.

Childline – 1098

CHILDLINE India Foundation (CIF) launched a toll free helpline CHILDLINE in 1996 to aid children in distress. The initiative is supported by the Union Ministry of Women and Child Development (MWCD) and focuses on street children who are victims of abuse. The toll free number 1098 is manned round the clock and operates in 291 cities or districts of the country providing support to children in need. Over 31 million calls have been attended to since inception making a great headway in the field of child safety and protection.

What Can I Do?

Report – Report all cases of suspected child abuse in your vicinity to the police, CHILDLINE, or the appropriate NGO for the safety and protection of the child/children involved.

Donate – Donate generously to NGOs such as the Akshaya Patra Foundation which help in providing midday meals to about 1.4 million children each day.

Volunteer – Volunteer to spend a few hours each week with Teach for India – a programme that aims at providing quality education to underprivileged children.

Promote – Promote the cause of girl children under programmes such as Beti Bachao Beti Padhao campaigns through your family and friends.

Connect – Connect with various NGOs and organisations working towards protection and safety of children in your neighbourhood.

FEMALE FETICIDE: CAUSES & EFFECTS OF SEX-SELECTIVE ABORTION

What is Female Feticide?

Female feticide is the selective abortion/elimination of the female child, done deliberately by the mother, after the detection of the child's gender through medical tests. This is usually done under familial pressure from the husband or the in-laws or even the woman's parents.

In places where cultural norms value male over female children (in India, China, Pakistan, the Caucasus, and Southeast Europe, for example), elective abortions of female fetuses are common. Like many societies around the world, India is patriarchal. A set hierarchy prevails in all tiers of its social order, and a fanatic preference for male children is especially common in India. From the ancient scriptures, one finds instances where men are glowingly praised as the key to continuing the family lineage, while females are forced to undergo multiple pregnancies and (or) abortions until they become breeding machines that produce male offspring.

Sadly, a majority of female feticide cases involve the enthusiastic participation of women, both old and young. To add fuel to the fire, the unethical sex determination and selective abortion of female infants has become a booming ($224 million US) industry. Money has become a dangerous incentive for this transgression.

Why Abort Female Fetuses?

Every unethical act has some lame age-old reasoning behind it which its staunch supporters use as justification. The cause of female feticide lies within the cultural norms as well as the socio-economic policies of the country where the practice prevails.

The most infected (I use the adjective "infected" because it precisely depicts the malady) are the South Asian countries like China, India, Vietnam, and Korea, but this social evil has mushroomed to western nations like the US and Canada. Immigration that has brought cultural preferences for female feticide across the pond. What is the rationale, one may wonder. Surprisingly, the reasons for killing female fetuses aren't quite as diverse as one may expect.

- "Male Children are a Better Investment." The main reason is the idea that the male offspring will better support the family. Since sons are seen as the main source of income, even though today, women have many career options, the common misconception still remains that it is the male who will help run the house and look after his parents, while women are viewed as being like cargo, something to be shipped off to another household.
- "Female Children Are a Gamble." In India, the age-old dowry system puts a damper on the spirits of those who are blessed with a girl child. When a girl is born, the parents begin to calculate the expense of her future marriage, the lump sum that will paid to the future groom's family. They worry that currency may depreciate and inflation may skyrocket. Because of this, the birth of a girl is seen as a tragedy waiting to happen.

- Women Don't Have Status in Society. As a result of institutional and cultural sexism, female children and adults have less power, status, rights, and money. Even as adults, it's harder for females to take care of or make decisions for themselves. Centuries of repression have made inferiority second nature to most women who have been taught the role of the meek, submissive, docile wife who works relentlessly to cater to the whims of her husband. Female feticide often happens with the explicit consent of the mother. Even the mothers-to-be agree to this misdeed out of an inherited cultural bias and a sense of duty to the family.
- Foul Medical Ethics. With the legalization of abortion in India, illegal sex determination and termination of pregnancies have become everyday realities. Professionals in the medical field are only too glad to help parents realize their dream of a healthy baby boy. Female feticide is openly discussed in the medical profession and many pin boards outside clinics have advertisements for abortion that read, "Pay Rs. 500 [$10 US] today to save the expense of Rs. 500 000 [$10,000 US] in the future." The cost of an abortion is nothing compared to the expense of having a child, especially a girl.
- Industrial Growth. Industrialization of the health sector has further established the practice of sex selective abortion. With the advent of CVS, amniocentesis, and ultrasound, sex determination of the fetus has become much easier. These manufacturers of high-tech equipment and gadgets benefit from the preference for male children. Many hospitals are known to sign long-term contracts with the firms involved in the production of these types of machines. Often, a healthy percentage of the profit is shared with the hospital, and both parties enjoy the fruits of rewarding a death sentence.

A Note on the Accuracy of Sex-Selective Abortions

As opposed to CVS and amniocentesis, ultrasound technology is cheaper and within easy reach of the lower economic strata of society. It is also easily accessible in a hospital/clinic nearby with mediocre credentials. Unfortunately, the accuracy of the ultrasound is not 100% until the fetus is twenty weeks old. Consequently, the children aborted by those enthusiastic parents may just be the little prince they were hoping for.

CAUSES OF FEMALE FOETICIDE

Various scholars have suggested different possible causes for the problem of female fortitude.

1. Low position of women: Women have been subjected to injustice since ages. Some people feel that the birth of girl child may lower their status in the society. There is an extreme desire for boy-child among some sections of our society.
2. Extreme poverty: People who live in extreme poor condition often think that the girl child would cause more economic hardship to them. The social evil of dowry system further worsens the situation. Some people think that they will to have to arrange for huge dowry for her marriage.
3. Illiteracy: Illiteracy is the leading of all social evils. Illiterate people are ignorant people, and not able to judge their actions in the right perspective.

How to save girl child?

1. Women empowerment: The women need to be empowered. A woman has every right to give birth to a baby. The girl child is a blessing of God. Just give her a chance, and she will make you proud with her achievements.
2. Awareness: Every citizen of civilized society should be made aware of the fact that a girl child is as important as a boy child. If she gets the right opportunity, she can provide economic support to the family and help them to come out of poverty level.
3. Education: Education raises the consciousness of a person. The mental pattern in favor of society should be transformed. This is the time for historic changes in the society.

How to save girl child after her birth?

The girl child is not only unsafe inside her mother's womb. Even after her birth, she has to face various hardships because of gender inequality. We must save the girl child after her birth as well.

1. We all agree that girls' education is very important. The girls should get a safe and comfortable environment at schools.
2. The girl should get equal access to the educational resources of the school.
3. There should be separate toilets for girl-children at schools.
4. There is need for a shift in mental attitude in favor of equality between boys and girls.
5. The family members of the girl child should come forward to protect her rights, both within and outside her home.
6. She should never be engaged as a child labor.
7. The physical abuse and harassment of girl child should be dealt strictly. The guilty should be punished as per the law.

Support

The 'save the child girl, educate the girl child' initiative is actively supported by the Government, corporate groups, human rights activists and NGOS.

Under the initiative of 'Beti Bachao Beti Padhao', several social organizations have come forward to build toilet at girl schools.

The corporate India, as part of their Corporate Social Responsibility (CSR), is also earmarking funds for the welfare of school going girls.

Legal status of prenatal sex determination

According to the laws prevailing in India, the determination of prenatal sex during pregnancy is illegal and punishable by law.

It is unfortunate that people still misuse the ultrasonography (diagnostic sonography) scan to determine the sex of the unborn baby. There is a need for:

1. Strict enforcement of laws relating to medical scanning.
2. Impart moral teachings on doctors.
3. Educate people that there is no difference between a girl and a boy child.

Conclusion

We belong to the modern generation of humanity. We seek an environment where every human-being is considered free. We seek an environment where every unborn child is welcomed without any gender bias.

Mahatma Gandhi gave the slogan of 'do or die' to his countrymen for the cause of their motherland. The unborn girl-child is also seeking similar spirit among the countrymen in support of her cause.

FEMALE FOETICIDE IN INDIA

Female foeticide in India is the act of killing a female foetus outside of the legal channels of abortion. It occurs in India for assumed cultural reasons that span centuries.

The frequency of female foeticide in India is assumed to be an estimation derived from its high birth sex ratio, that is the ratio of boys to girls at birth. The natural ratio is assumed to be between 103 to 107, and any number above it is considered as suggestive of female foeticide. According to the decennial Indian census, the sex ratio in the 0 to 6 age group in India has risen from 102.4 males per 100 females in 1961, to 104.2 in 1980, to 107.5 in 2001, to 108.9 in 2011.

The child sex ratio is within the normal natural range in all eastern and southern states of India, but significantly higher in certain western and particularly northwestern states such as Punjab, Haryana and Jammu & Kashmir (118, 120 and 116, as of 2011, respectively). The western states of Maharashtra and Rajasthan 2011 census found a child sex ratio of 113, Gujarat at 112 and Uttar Pradesh at 111.

The Indian census data suggests there is a positive correlation between abnormal sex ratio and better socio-economic status and literacy. This may be connected to the dowry system in India where dowry deaths occur when a girl is seen as a financial burden. Urban India has higher child sex ratio than rural India according to 1991, 2001 and 2011 Census data, implying higher prevalence of female foeticide in urban India. Similarly, child sex ratio greater than 115 boys per 100 girls is found in regions where the predominant majority is Hindu, Muslim, Sikh or Christian; furthermore "normal" child sex ratio of 104 to 106 boys per 100 girls are also found in regions where the predominant majority is Hindu, Muslim, Sikh or Christian. These data contradict any hypotheses that may suggest that sex selection is an archaic practice which takes place among uneducated, poor sections or particular religion of the Indian society.

There is an ongoing debate as to whether these high sex ratios are only caused by female foeticide or some of the higher ratio is explained by natural causes. The Indian government has passed Pre-Conception and Pre-Natal Diagnostic Techniques Act (PCPNDT) in 1994 to ban and punish prenatal sex screening and female foeticide. It is currently illegal in India to determine or disclose sex of the foetus to anyone. However, there are concerns that PCPNDT Act has been poorly enforced by authorities.

High sex ratio implications

One school of scholars suggest that any birth sex ratio of boys to girls that is outside of the normal 105-107 range, necessarily implies sex-selective abortion. These scholars claim that both the sex ratio at birth and the population sex ratio are remarkably constant in human populations. Significant deviations in birth sex ratios from the normal range can only be explained by manipulation, that is sex-selective abortion. In a widely cited article, Amartya Sen compared the birth sex ratio in Europe (106) and United States (105) with those in Asia (107+) and argued that the high sex ratios in East Asia, West Asia and South Asia may be due to excessive female mortality. Sen pointed to research that had shown that if men and women receive similar nutritional and medical attention and good health care then females have better survival rates, and it is the male which is the genetically fragile sex. Sen estimated 'missing women' from extra women who would have survived in Asia if it had the same ratio of women to men as Europe and United States. According to Sen, the high birth sex ratio over decades, implies a female shortfall of 11% in Asia, or over 100 million women as missing from the 3 billion combined population of India, other South Asian countries, West Asia, North Africa and China.

High human sex ratio may be natural

Other scholars question whether birth sex ratio outside 103-107 can be due to natural reasons. William James and others suggest that conventional assumptions have been:

- there are equal numbers of X and Y chromosomes in mammalian sperms
- X and Y stand equal chance of achieving conception
- therefore equal number of male and female zygotes are formed, and that
- therefore any variation of sex ratio at birth is due to sex selection between conception and birth.

James cautions that available scientific evidence stands against the above assumptions and conclusions. He reports that there is an excess of males at birth in almost all human populations, and the natural sex ratio at birth is usually between 102 to 108. However the ratio may deviate significantly from this range for natural reasons such as early marriage and fertility, teenage mothers, average maternal age at birth, paternal age, age gap between father and mother, late births, ethnicity, social and economic stress, warfare, environmental and harmonal effects. This school of scholars support their alternate hypothesis with historical data when modern sex-selection technologies were unavailable, as well as birth sex ratio in sub-regions, and various ethnic groups of developed economies. They suggest that direct abortion data should be collected and studied, instead of drawing conclusions indirectly from human sex ratio at birth.

James hypothesis is supported by historical birth sex ratio data before technologies for ultrasonographic sex-screening were discovered and commercialized in 1960s and 1970s, as well by reverse abnormal sex ratios currently observed in Africa. Michel Garenne reports that many African nations have, over decades, witnessed birth sex ratios below 100, that is more girls are born than boys.

Angola, Botswanaand Namibia have reported birth sex ratios between 94 to 99, which is quite different than the presumed 104 to 106 as natural human birth sex ratio.

South Korea's historical records suggest a birth sex ratio of 1.13, based on 5 million births, in 1920s over a 10-year period.Other historical records from Asia too support James hypothesis. For example, Jiang et al. claim that the birth sex ratio in China was 116–121 over a 100-year period in late 18th and early 19th century; in the 120–123 range in early 20th century; falling to 112 in the 1930s.

Origin

Female foeticide has been linked to the arrival, in the early 1990s, of affordable ultrasound technology and its widespread adoption in India.Obstetric ultrasonography, either transvaginally or transabdominally, checks for various markers of fetal sex. It can be performed at or after week 12 of pregnancy.

At this point, $^{3}D_{4}$ of fetal sexes can be correctly determined, according to a 2001 study. Accuracy for males is approximately 50% and for females almost 100%. When performed after week 13 of pregnancy, ultrasonography gives an accurate result in almost 100% of cases.

Availability

Ultrasound technology arrived in China and India in 1979, but its expansion was slower in India. Ultrasound sex discernment technologies were first introduced in major cities of India in 1980s, its use expanded in India's urban regions in 1990s, and became widespread in 2000s.

Magnitude estimates for female foeticide

Estimates for female foeticide vary by scholar. One group estimates more than 10 million female foetuses may have been illegally aborted in India since 1990s, and 500,000 girls were being lost annually due to female foeticide. MacPherson estimates that 100,000 abortions every year continue to be performed in India solely because the fetus is female.

DISAPPEARING DAUGHTERS: FEMALE FETICIDE IN INDIA

Mitu Khurana, a Delhi pediatrician, claims she was tricked into a sex determination test by her husband. Her husband and in laws abused her verbally and physically so that she would abort the twin girls she was carrying. Mitu refused, moved to her parents' house and filed a case against her husband under the PCPNDT (Pre Conception and Pre Natal Diagnostic Techniques) Act. "An official told me I'm wasting my youth and my life," she recalls. "Just give him a son if he wants one, they said." (Khurana's story is told in the documentary, *It's a Girl.*) Suvarna Gaikwad's husband and her mother-in-law kicked, punched and 'stomped on' her belly after they were told she was having a baby girl. When she refused to have an abortion, they savagely attacked her. The husband, mother-in-law and two others stomped on her stomach, killing the unborn baby, which had to be aborted. Three-month-old Hina was admitted to a hospital's intensive care unit struggling for survival. Hina's father Umar Farooq confessed trying to kill his daughter. Reshma Banu, Hina's anguished mother, recalled how her husband Umar sent her to buy biscuits and then stuffed poison-laced food into the infant's mouth to get rid of her.

Sadly, the murder of the girl child, whether as a fetus, or immediately after birth, has reached epidemic proportions in India. Female feticide, or the selective abortion of a female fetus for no other crime but being a female, is becoming increasingly common. A strange combination of patriarchal attitudes and access to modern medical procedures have made it a menace of comparable magnitude to poverty or malnutrition, as the numbers will demonstrate. Whether seen from a purely moral, or a purely pragmatic point of view, this type of violence on women has the potential to create tremendous demographic and social turmoil in the near future. One of India's oldest and crudest means to alter the gender composition of children, i.e., female infanticide relies on a set of procedures to kill girls within a few days after their birth. Techniques vary locally according to indigenous know-how and available resources (such as local poisonous plants). Such techniques have also evolved spontaneously over the years, incorporating newly available elements (such as pesticide). Horrifyingly, infanticide's "efficiency" is beyond doubt, and its financial cost is also extremely limited because of its reliance on local resources. Another disgustingly effective and more common practice is neglect. It consists of a passive strategy intended to deprive girls of fair access to and share of resources, with a reduced probability of survival as a consequence.

In recent years, sex-selective abortion has become another technique to murder girls, using pre-natal sex determination. Pre-natal diagnostic techniques involve two main technologies, i.e. amniocentesis and ultrasonography. In India, pre-natal sex determination relies mostly on the latter, a non-invasive technology that is also easier and cheaper to conduct than amniocentesis. Most physicians are largely conscious of the ethical implications of this technology and are opposed to sex selection. However, as always, a small number of unscrupulous practitioners have become rich by performing illegal sex diagnoses or sex-selective abortions, given the strong social bias towards boys.

In traditional Indian culture, the female, and especially the mother is revered and there are significant female oriented religious cults and observances in the dominant Indian religion, ie Hinduism. However, there have always been significant restrictions on the freedom of a woman in all major Indian religious traditions. The Manusamhita, which tends to drive traditional Hindu rituals and accompanied behavior in Northern India, clearly specifies an inferior role for women as a whole, and specially wives. While the Independence Movement earlier and the Indian Constitution later codified formal equality of men and women, the laws are often very difficult to implement.

In the context of a deeply conservative social structure, enforcing women's rights runs right into the patriarchal views of the larger society. For example, even though dowry, a practice where parents of brides have to pay large gifts to the groom's family, has been outlawed, there has been very little prosecution over the years.

In a traditionalist, agrarian society where the vast majority of Indians still live today, children are viewed as sources of labor and future income. Male children are valued since they can perform physical labor, and will likely fetch a dowry at time of marriage. Daughters are physically weaker, socially restricted from performing labor, and may offer the prospect of severe financial hardship for families at the time of weddings (cost of weddings are usually borne by the bride's family). By this view, poor rural families are likely to have the highest rates of female feticide.

The reality, as usual, is complex. The five lowest states by sex ratio in India are Haryana, Jammu & Kashmir, Sikkim, Punjab & Uttar Pradesh. By per capita income, the poorest states are Bihar, Uttar Pradesh, Jharkhand, Manipur & Assam. Interestingly, Punjab & Haryana are among the wealthiest states by per capita income, suggesting that it is not just economic deprivation that causes families to kill their girl children. In fact, the so-called Northern Hindi belt states are all below the national average, while all the Southern states are above; it provides anecdotal evidence to us that culture, and not just economic deprivation, plays a significant role in the attitude towards women.

Ironically, the increase in female feticide in India is likely a sad side effect of material progress, as well as aided by policies that would normally enhance women's rights. Abortion was legalized in India in 1971 allowing for abortion in the case of rape, genetic abnormalities for the child, physical/mental health of the woman, as well as failure of birth control devices adopted by the parents. In practice, it is almost entirely at the discretion of the medical professional involved. Also, given the widespread fears about India's rapidly rising population, there have been very few practical restrictions on abortion rights. The door was opened for sex-selective abortion in India and the ability to detect genetic abnormalities via medical ultrasound in the child also yielded sex data. My view is that relative affluence, without any accompanying progressive attitudes towards women, have exacerbated the trend towards female feticide. This is the reason as culturally conservative states such as Punjab & Haryana, as well as their much poorer cousins such as Uttar Pradesh & Bihar, have the highest rates of female feticide.

Sex selection appears to have played a major role in causing the deterioration observed in child sex ratio. Excess female mortality among infants and children contributes only moderately to the deficit of girls. The Indian Medical Association estimates that five million female fetuses are aborted each year. India's child sex ratio (0-6 years) has declined from 945 in 1991 to 927 in 2001 and now to the lowest since independence: 914 females per 1,000 males in 2011. Overall sex ratios in the national capital New Delhi, and two adjacent states Punjab & Haryana are below 900 per 1,000 males as of the 2011 census.

An unbalanced sex ratio, specially in the northern states, has serious implications on social stability. We can foresee gender-related crime growing; the traditional family structure disturbed; the proliferation of prostitution and crimes against women as well as acceleration in the growth of sexually transmitted diseases and AIDS. To us, it is not a surprise that India has been experiencing a tremendous upsurge in violence against women, especially rape. As men see women as the vulnerable group who are a becoming numerically smaller, and the prospects for marriage recede, the incidence of gang rapes can only rise. The rise of forced marriages and bride buying which are common in North India may also be a result of female feticide. Since there aren't enough local women to marry, Haryana's (sex ratio 877 per 1,000 men) men pay touts to bring women for them to marry and to work on their farms. Social activists believe most of these women end up being used as sex slaves and then resold to other men in what looks like a flourishing market in trafficking of women.

After years of ignoring the problem, both mass media and government have begun to realize the larger implications of murdering girl children. The Indian Medical Association (IMA) and the Medical Council of India (MCI) have come out openly against the practice of sex-determination by some members of the medical fraternity. The PCPNDT (Pre Conception and Pre-natal

Diagnostic Technique Act) which banned pre-natal sex determination, provides the tools to act against the misuse of technology but also requires a pronounced effort from local authorities. Initial attempts to use legal means to prosecute unscrupulous doctors who assisted in sex determination and subsequent abortions only scratched the surface of the problem. The Government launched in 2011 a "Save the Girl Child Campaign" and is trying to lessen the preference for a son by highlighting the achievements of young girls.

The PNDT (Pre conception and Pre Natal Diagnostic Techniques) Act in India which was implemented in 1994 and later amended in 2002 bans pre natal sex determination with a view to prevent sex selective abortion. So unlike in the USA, sex determination during pregnancy is illegal.

In our view, the issue of female infanticide or feticide is related to the larger issue of gender equality and respect. Female feticide cannot be combated simply by a legalistic approach. All the best-intentioned campaigns or laws will be completely irrelevant unless society as a whole learns to treat women with respect. India has never had a strong feminist movement, and it is still common for women to completely defer to their father or husband for making crucial life decisions such as marriage, career, children etc. Unless the entire mindset of society improves, and with it the position of women, only very terrible consequences can result from the continuing violence that the women of India face from birth, and sometimes even before they are born.

THE IMPORTANCE OF SECURITY IN INDIAN SCHOOLS

Indian schools are notoriously low on security and many schools across the country are yet to install world class security arrangements.

Many crimes relating to children are occurring and criminals find it easy to kidnap children from schools using several different ploys.

However, in recent times schools have realized the importance of having a proper security arrangement and this is being put into place, albeit a little slowly. Some of aspects that schools have to consider are as follows:

Schools Buses

Students are often kidnapped when they are waiting to embark a school bus and this is one of the primary problems that parents and schools are facing. Some schools are planning to opt for a GPS tracking device on their school buses and the parents will also receive text messages every time the child embarks or disembarks the bus. This is not a fool proof method; however it is a useful way for schools and parents to monitor the movement of the buses. This solution can be implemented only on school owned buses and many students travel to and from their houses on private vans and vehicles and it is extremely difficult to track the movement of these.

School Security

Most private schools have security personnel stationed at the gate and they are usually hired from a security agency. Schools have to ensure that the security agency is trustworthy and parents can check this aspect before admitting their children in a school. Most schools require people who enter the school premises to register their names and phone numbers. Schools should also monitor the performance of the security guards.

This is primarily important for boarding schools as the children are on campus for a majority of the day. Boarding schools are also usually set away from the city and this makes the security arrangement much more important. Boarding schools usually have huge support staffs who are assigned the task of dealing with internal security.

Most boarding schools have constant patrols and everyone who enters is registered and escorted to the appropriate buildings. Parents are encouraged to check on these security arrangements beforehand.

Internal Security

Recently, many cases of child molestation have come to light and teachers are almost always the main culprits in these cases.

In a boarding school, where children spend most of the time alone with teachers, one cannot be sure whether children are being ill treated. Schools must ensure that they run a background check on all staff and this includes, both teaching and non teaching staff. Internal security is managed by peons and in case of a residential school by the hostel warden. Residential schools that are meant for girls generally employ women staff for teaching and the wardens are also women.

Attendance

Constant checking of a student's attendance is one of the best ways to be able to maintain proper security in a school. The security guards at the gate must be instructed to not permit anyone outside the gate without the permission of the school principal. This will ensure that children are kept safe during class hours. Security arrangements in Indian schools are improving, however there is scope for more improvement and parents are advised to check the security arrangements thoroughly before enrolling their children.

ARE THE CHILDREN SAFE IN OUR SCHOOLS?

We send our children to the school to get educated, and till a few decades ago, we did not have to dwell too much on the safety of our children in the schools; we took it for granted, for the school was always synonymous with the word 'safe'. Unfortunately, it is no longer the case.

In 1995, in Mandi Dabwali, many school children perished in a fire at a prize distribution ceremony

In 2001, 971 school children died in the Bhuj earthquake

In 2004, 94 children burned to death in a school in Kumbakonam

In 2013, 24 children died of food poisoning after the mid-day meal in a Bihar school

In 2014, a 6-year old child was raped by two gym instructors.

The list seems to be endless; from natural calamities to the man-made ones, from the negligence of man to the beast like action of man, our children are no longer safe in school. Some of these disasters could have been averted by simple prevention and preparedness. We, as parents, must make certain that we are aware of the norms and regulations that a school must follow, and keep a vigil on their compliance. The recent terror attack on a school in Pakistan should jolt the parents of school going children in India out of their complacency, and they should become more aware.

Disaster management in schools

Creating a safe environment for the children in school is the most important task, as in the case of any emergency they are the most vulnerable. National Disaster Management Authority, of the Ministry of Home Affairs, strongly feels that there has to be a structural, as well as non-structural intervention, to ensure the safety of the children. Structural intervention would include strict check on the guidelines set up for school buildings, while non-structural would mean educating the staff, teachers, and students about disaster management. The Ministry insists that every school adopt a school safety programme targeting the educational institutions, emergency officials, teachers, students and even the community at large. Under this programme, the students learn about safety measures, thus becoming future disaster managers, while a disaster resilient society is built by way of educating the community. Some of the ways and means of educating the child are:

- Building awareness by way of campaigns, rallies etc
- Conducting mock drills for fire disasters and earthquakes
- First aid training
- A clear picture of command and control, so that in case of an emergency there is no chaos
- Use of the fire extinguisher.

With terror attacks on schools all over the world, India should also prepare itself for any such eventualities. The schools must take necessary precautions against entry of unknown individuals to schools by issuing an identity card even for the parents. The security checks should be strict. The students may be given some tips as to how to behave in a hostage situation by professional counsellors.

Keep the child's childhood safe

Child molestation and rape in schools has sadly become very common and an everyday news. In fact, after the rape of a 6-year old in a school in Bangalore, many schools have abdicated their responsibility, both legal and ethical, towards the children. A parent in Bangalore received the following form from her child's school, for signature:

It stated: "In consideration of my child's participation in various events organised by the school, I hereby release the management, officers, employees and agents of the school, its parent and sister concerns and any other people officially connected with the events from any and all liability for damage to or loss of personal property, sickness or injury from whatever source, legal entanglements, loss of life or money, which might occur while the child is participating in the event."

Thus as parents we need to step forward and ensure the safety of our children and see to it that their childhood is not snatched away from them. We need to do the following:

- Educate the child; as per the age, teach the child the difference between good touch and bad touch.
- Convince the child, no matter what, our love for them is unconditional
- Open all channels of communication with the child
- Create a buddy system in school, so that the child is always in the company of a friend. Each should know the whereabouts of the other at all times
- Regularly interact with teachers, including physical education and art teacher; make it a point to immediately meet any newly appointed teacher.

Activists and parents feel that it should be mandatory for schools across the country to have a child protection policy, or CPP, in place. CPP protects the child from abuse, harm, neglect and exploitation of any nature. As of now, CPP has been adopted only by the State of Delhi, based on the guidelines of the Delhi Commission for Protection of Child Rights.

CONSEQUENCES OF FEMALE FOETICIDE IN INDIA

Female foeticide has a serious impact on the society, in the overall growth and development of the country. Let us discuss below the effects of female foeticide in India:

Skewed sex ratio: According to 2011 census, the child sex ratio in India was 919 females to 1000 males, which declined from 927 females to 1000 males in the previous decade. Haryana, which is supposed to be one of the richest states in India, takes the top most position in skewed sex ratio. Other prominent states are Punjab, Delhi, Gujarat, Maharashtra, Himachal Pradesh, Rajasthan, Uttar Pradesh etc. Skewed sex ratios are seen in almost all the states of India, except in North East India and some of South India. Since 1991, more than 80% of districts in India have shown a reducing sex ratio. Going by this, the next census by 2022 will definitely show a further reduction in sex ratios all over the country. It is horrifying to state that illegal foetal sex determination and sex selective abortion have developed into a Rs. 1000 crore industry in India.

Killing a girl child before or after she is born has an adverse effect on the sex ratio and leads to further social evils. Skewed sex ratio, which is the result of female foeticide, has other negative consequences in the society.

Shortage of girls for marriage: "Baljeet Singh, a truck driver of Haryana, gave up hope of finding a girl for his marriage from his state Haryana. He was 30. He then got married to a young girl, half of his age, from a Muslim community in Assam"

In a recent report by the Red Cross Society, there is a large number of bachelors who have crossed the marriageable age in Punjab and Haryana because of shortage of girls.

Eligible Jat boys from Haryana are seeking brides from areas which are far away from their home town, like Kerala, to change their "single" status to "married". These are just a few instances.

With fewer women, it is interesting to notice the "Indian marriage market". Men are willing to pay a large amount of money to get married to a girl from other states like Jharkhand, Bihar, West Bengal, or Madhya Pradesh. The outcome is that while the parents of the girls benefit, the girls themselves have to compromise their culture, dress, language and food habits.

Trafficking and prostitution: Girls are kidnapped or stolen. They are sold and resold at varied prices. Eventually, they end up being prostitutes. Increasing number of child marriages: Many women from poverty zones or poverty-stricken families get married before 18 years in order to survive and prevent being a burden to the family. The number of child marriage is increasing. Girls get married to men double their age. They are forced to get married to old men.

Increasing maternal deaths and ill-health of women: Killing of a foetus in the womb or abortion weakens the health of a woman. In some cases, the women have to undergo many abortions till they conceive a male child. The outcome is that there is an increasing number of maternal deaths. Women undergoing abortions are also more prone to infections and sickness.

Increase in polyandry: Munni, a young woman came, to Baghpat village, UP as a young bride, years ago. She was then forced to have sex with her two unmarried brothers-in-law and bear children from them as well. Today she is the mother of 3 sons from her husband and his brothers. Munni is still "unhappily married" but she has not filed any complaint.

There are many such incidents happening in India. In most villages in India where female foeticide is practiced, one wife lives with many unmarried brothers.

5

Education of Girls

In Article 15(1) the Constitution of India, on the right to equality, provides the basic policy framework that enshrines the vision of girls' education and the spirit in which their education is to be provided. Article 45 of the Constitution refers to "free and compulsory education for all children" up to 14 years but this 'directive principle' could not be enforced in court. The Right of Children to Free and Compulsory Education Act adopted in 2009, however, now legally requires states to provide free education to children aged 6 to 14 and reserves 25 per cent of private primary school places for disadvantaged children.

Moreover, recently public funding has attached weight to poverty-related factors, including deficits in education. Before 2007, equity played only a limited role in allocating resources for education. A new formula attaches more weight to social indicators, including a district-level Education Development Index. In 2005-06 the differences in per child allocation between high and low Education Development Index districts were negligible, but in 2008-09 districts in the lowest 25 per cent on the index received twice as much per child as those in the highest 25 per cent. Combined gross enrolment in education in India was in 2006 overall 61.0 per cent: females 57.4 per cent, males 64.3 per cent – or a women to parity of 89 per cent.

At first sight India seems on track to achieve the Millennium Development Goal of Universal Primary Education by 2015, especially if one realises that India has come from far. Only about

55 per cent of the population born between 1950 and 1970 attended primary school or higher. According to the MICS 2000 survey, almost 27 million school-age children in India did not attend school, or one out of four; girls made up a majority of 57 per cent. At the time, India's exclusion rate was 15 per cent, meaning that this proportion of children would likely never attend school.

Against this backdrop, in 2001 the central government launched the Sarva Shiksha Abhiyan programme to provide elementary education for all of India's children. SSA is one of India's first major programmes to cover upper primary education –grades 6-8—as well. The programme aims to enroll all 6-14 year-olds in school by 2015, retain them in school, and provide them with quality education at least till grade 8 – a tougher requirement than meeting the MDG by 2015 as such. Most international comparative sources give a rather rosy picture of progress thus far. Because of a substantial increase in girls' net enrollment rate in primary education, the total net enrollment rate in primary education increased from 84.9 per cent in 1991 to an overall 88 per cent over 2000-2007, divided into 90 per cent for boys and 87 per cent for girls, or 97 per cent girls to boys parity.

The UN MDG Indicators even indicate for 2006 a net primary enrollment rate of 94.3 per cent, divided into 96.1 per cent for boys and 92.2 per cent for girls. For 2007, primary net enrollment was set at 90 per cent: 91 per cent for boys and 88 per cent for girls, implying that nine of ten children of primary school age attended primary school. Yet, there are two caveats. First, domestic sources suggest less reasons for optimism. The 2005-06 National Family Health Survey outcomes are a much lower primary net enrollment rate, namely 83 per cent; 85 per cent for boys and 81 per cent for girls, as well as gaps between urban and rural areas, and especially between socio-economics groups, with 96 per cent of children from the wealthiest 20 per cent of the population attending primary school, versus only 69 per cent of children from the poorest 20 per cent families.

Second, another important indicator concerning primary educational advancement is the primary completion rate, taking account of drop-outs and indicating which share of the children who have enrolled in the first grade of primary education can be expected to reach the last grade. This gives a more realistic picture of actual school attendance. Unless impressive progress in many educational fields, the Indian drop-out rates are still comparatively high: in 2005-06 25.5 per cent in primary schools, 48.7 per cent in secondary schools, and 61.6 per cent in secondary schools. Consequently, with 65.8 per cent in 2005-06 the overall primary completion rate remained low, though girls' rate had hardly any gap left compared to boys'. For India, "the big challenge is keeping children in school once they enroll".

The most recent UNESCO report concludes that India's wealth divides in education are among the largest in the world – and that they are reinforced by regional and gender disparities. The report states that in 2005 over three in 10 Indian females aged 17 to 22 were in "education poverty", meaning that they had fewer than four years of education, nearly double the proportion of males of the same age. Another source concludes for 2005-06 that 37 per cent of Indian females aged 15 to 19 had less than six years of education: 45 per cent in the rural areas against 19 per cent in the urban areas. In Bihar this share was even 61 per cent, in Jharkhand 56 per cent, and in Chhattisgarh and Uttar Pradesh both 45 per cent. By contrast, in Kerala only 2 per cent of all adolescent females had less than six years of education, in Himachal Pradesh 7 per cent, in Goa 8 per cent, in Tamil Nadu 12 per cent, and in Maharashtra 17 per cent.

Living and health conditions of the poor are highly relevant here. Child malnutrition seriously hampers cognitive development. Drawing on unique research that tracks children in four developing countries — including India— through their early years, marked nutrition-related disadvantages in test scores at age 4 to 5 have been revealed. By age 7 to 8, the malnutrition penalty is equivalent to the loss of a full term of schooling. And in India in 2000-07 nearly two in five children were stunted: many of them will carry a burden of disadvantage into primary school.

Moreover, the available figures imply that 17 per cent or 21 million children of primary school age in India were out of school in 2006. Compared to 2000, the number of such children had decreased by six million. Yet, the MDG UPE goal for 2015 can only be met if the increase in primary school attendance accelerates in the years to come, especially among the poor. It should be noted that in 2005 children from the poorest 20 per cent were over three times more likely to be out of school than children from the richest 20 per cent. Children with disabilities are heavily disadvantaged. According to a World Bank analysis of India's 2002 National Sample Survey, children with disabilities were 5.5 times more likely to be out of school.

Almost three-quarters of children with severe impairments were out of school. The most likely to be excluded were children with mental illness or blindness. In 2007, the gross enrollment rate in secondary education was 57 per cent, again considerable progress as this rate was in 1981 only 33 per cent, in 1993 41 per cent, in 1999 48 per cent and in 2005-06 54 per cent.

Moreover, over these years girls of secondary school age diminished the gender gap considerably. In 1991, women to men parity in secondary education was just 60 per cent, which improved to 69 per cent in 1999; in the 2000s the closing of the gender gap speeded up, with 83 per cent parity in 2005-06 till in 2007 85 per cent parity was reached, through gross enrollment rates of 61 per cent for males and 52 per cent for females. In the 1990s and 2000s the expansion of India's IT/BPO.

Nevertheless, with both a relatively low gross enrollment rate and a relatively low women to men parity India does not compare favourably to other many Asian countries. Its results do not match the rule that Asian women study longer than Asian men, and its 2005-06 women to men parity ratio of 83 per cent in secondary education was one of the lowest ratios of 41 Asian economies.

Currently the composition of the 40 million children enrolled in secondary education is skewed towards the urban areas and even heavier towards children from the wealthier classes: 83 per cent of children from the wealthiest 20 per cent of the population attend secondary school, against only 29 per cent of children from the poorest 20 per cent families and 43 per cent of children from the second poorest 20 per cent.

Also, secondary school enrollment varies widely across states, from 92 per cent in Kerala to 22 per cent in Bihar and only 4 per cent in Jharkhand. The World Bank argues that actually with larger numbers of children finishing primary school, the demand for secondary schooling –grades 9 to 12—is growing. Over the next decade an increasing share of these students will come from rural and lower income groups, who will be less able to afford private secondary education. Against this backdrop, the World Bank points at the risks of the situation that 60 per cent of India's secondary school system is privately managed. The Indian technical and vocational education system is still in its infancy, and difficult to access for females.

By 2005, in the group 15-29 of age 6.8 million males and 4.3 million females were receiving or had received formal vocational training. Another 14.2 million males and 8.1 million females received informal training; as to be expected, this kind of training dominates in the unorganised sector. Jointly, the categories of formal and informal trained made up only about 11.5 per cent of this age group in the labour force: 14 per cent of the young males and 9 per cent of the young females; for only the formally trained this share was 3.7 per cent — a level with which India compares poorly across countries. The country's Industrial Training Institutes and various craft centres are not accessible to the vast majority of the poor.

Moreover, the gender disparities reported in TVET are large, with girls accounting for just 7 per cent of enrollment at the secondary level and their courses concentrated in traditional areas such as nursing and sewing. In general, the benefits of vocational training are not immediately apparent. Some 60 per cent of graduates from ITIs are still unemployed three years later, also because they do not derive benefits in entry to higher technical education courses. Industrial apprentices are more likely to get work, but generally not in the trade for which they trained. The career paths of TVET teachers are uncertain and uninspiring, and public awareness of the potential of TVET is very limited. Governance problems have hampered India's efforts to strengthen vocational education.

Duplication and fragmentation are widespread, there is little control over quality and the certification system is poorly understood by employers. Companies and employer organisations are only marginally involved, though efforts are being made to strengthen their engagement. Moreover, formal retraining of adult workers is virtually absent. Only 16 per cent of Indian manufacturers offer in-service training compared to over 90 per cent in China. The relative position of India's women is also lagging behind in tertiary education, where in 2006-07 the country's women to men enrollment ratio was 67 per cent.

It cannot be denied that in 1991, with a women / men ratio of 54 per cent, the situation was even worse for girls and young women, but between 1991 and 2007 India's progress has remained comparatively limited. In 2007, 13 per cent of the 17-25 of age were enrolled in tertiary education: 16 per cent of the young men of that age, and 11 per cent of the young females.

Enrollment increases quickly. In 2006-07, the massive amount of 13,93 million students was enrolled in institutions of higher education, as against 11,78 million in 2005-06; 4,47 million were female, constituting 40.4 per cent or a 67 per cent women to men parity rate.

In 2004-05 female Ph.D's, D.Sc's and D.Phill's made up 41 per cent of this category; female MA's made up 47 per cent of all MA's, and female MSc's 46 per cent of all MSc's. As such, the growth of India's higher education system is impressive.

The Eleventh Five-Year Plan outlines major expansion plans, including funding for 30 new Central Universities, five new Indian Institutes of Science, Education and Research, eight new Indian Institutes of Technology, seven new Indian Institutes of Management and 20 new Indian Institutes of Information Technology.

Qualitative progress is impressive too. The top students of the Indian Institutes for Technology, for example, are already not just globally competive, in many ways they set the global standard – with many alumni careering in California's Silicon Valley and elsewhere in the US.

Also, recent graduates of Indian Institutes of Management are so in demand that already in 2006 their very top salaries approached about USD 225,000. Yet, besides praising such academic progress a World Bank Policy Review stressed the related societal contradictions. To cite just one example of many: "Delhi's new metro is a 21st century marvel while rural roads in many states are in poor repair and often impassable". Another World Bank report, regarding innovation in India, also emphasizes these striking societal disparities and contradictions. The report argues that inclusive innovation, and improved knowledge absorption, can play a critical role in lowering the costs of goods and services and in creating income-earning opportunities for the poor.

GIRLS EDUCATION IN INDIA : ACHIEVEMENTS SINCE INDEPENDENCE

The leaders of our freedom movement realized the importance of girls' education and had put it as a prime agenda for national development. However, when India attained independence some 60 years ago, it was a formidable challenge that the new government had to face. The national female literacy rate was an alarmingly low 8.9 per cent, Gross Enrolment Ratio (GER) for girls was 24.8 per cent at primary level and 4.6 per cent at the upper primary level (in the 11 – 14 years age group). Social and cultural barriers to education of women and lack of access to organized schooling, had to be addressed immediately.

ACCESS TO SCHOOLING IMPROVED

Education administrators gave high priority on reducing the infrastructure/access deficiency. Focused attention on this need has resulted in establishing a network of 7,67,520 schools at the primary level and 2,74,731 schools at the upper primary level by 2004-05 from just 2,09,671 primary and 13,596 upper primary schools in 1950-51. A large majority (87%) of these are rural schools. Today 98 per cent of India's rural population has access to primary schools within a kilometer of the habitation.

Greater access to schooling is, however, not enough. Special measures are called for to help girls join the schools. These include setting up of girls toilets and providing separate girls' schools at upper primary level to counter community resistance to girls' studying in co-educational schools. Some schools are residential ones – the recent addition to residential schools being the Kasturba Gandhi Balika Vidyalayas that target the most disadvantaged girls at the upper primary stage.

The Government continues to be the major provider of elementary education with 90.2 per cent primary and 72.2 per cent upper primary schools managed either by Government or by local bodies. Annual maintenance grants and school improvement grants are being provided to each school at the elementary level.

Upswing In Girls' Enrolment

Growth in access to schooling has been matched by a steady increase in enrolment with the most dramatic upswing since 1990s in girls participation levels. From 13.8 million boys and 5.4 million girls enrolled at the primary level in 1950-51, the number rose to 69.7 million boys and 61.1 million girls in 2004-05. At the upper primary level, the enrolment increased from 2.6 million boys and 0.5 million girls to 28.5 million boys and 22.7 million girls.

The proportion of girls in the total enrolment has also been growing. Girls' enrolment at the primary stage increased from 28.1% in 1950-51 to 46.7% in 2004-05. At the upper primary stage, girls' enrolment rose from 16.1% in 1950-51 to 44.4% in 2004-05. The overall improvement in girls' enrolment with respect to total population of girls clearly shows that there is a near universal enrolment at primary level. The gap and challenge exists now at upper primary stage, but there too the gap is narrowing steadily.

Enrolment of Scheduled Caste and Scheduled Tribe girls poses a greater challenge to India's education administrators. Survey data, however, revealed that the participation of these disadvantaged girls in basic education, has grown steadily over the years. G.E.R. for SC girls at primary level have climbed up from 64.8% in 1986-87 to 106.6% in 2004-05 and at upper primary stage, from as low as 26.6% in 1986-87 to 61.5%in 2004-05. In the case of ST girls, the GER at primary level have gone up from 68% in 1986-87 to 115.5% by 2004-05 and from 21.9% in 1986-87 to

59.5% in 2004-05 for upper primary level. The overall gender gap in enrolment at the primary stage has dropped to 4.6 percentage points and that at the upper primary level has reduced to 8.0 percentage points in 2005. There are only 48 districts out of a total of 600 districts in India, with a gender gap above 10 percentage points at the primary stage. Focused attention is being targeted to these districts by education policy planners, in order to address the barriers in specific terms.

Declining Drop Out Rates And Out Of School Girls

Providing access and enrolment to schooling facilities are only a part of the story. Our aim is also to help the students to continue their studies. Although the phenomenon of drop outs continue to be a serious problem in India's education scenario, the drop out rates in elementary education have been on the decline, more sharply so for girls. Girls drop out rate in 2004-05 was lower than for boys, at primary level *i.e* 25.42% compared to 31.81% for boys. Since 2000, girls drop out rates have fallen by 16.5% points in just four years, compared to a reduction of only 4.1% points over the entire last decade (1990-2000).

With respect to the situation inside the school it is found that the repetition rates have been fast declining for girls. Two clear messages that underlie this trend are: one, that girls who enter the school system do not leave easily and two, school efficiency is gradually improving with girls completing the elementary cycle of education in lesser time. The number of out of school children have also been declining rapidly, from 32 million in 2001-02 to 7.5 million in 2006-07. Of the total age cohort of girls in the 6-14 years age group, 3.9% are reportedly out of school. In the 6-11 years age group, out of school girls are 3.34 percent and in the 11-14 years age group they are 5.3 percent. The inclusion of these 'hard to reach' and older girls, who have remained excluded from the education net is being addressed through context specific strategies and interventions presently.

More Girls Move To Upper Primary

The trends in transition rates from Primary to Upper Primary are also positive. The transition rate has improved from 71.98 in

2003 to 80.64 in 2005. The gains in the transition rates of girls (8.6 percentage points) have been higher than that of boys (7.65 percentage points). This has led to sharper decline in the gender gap in transition rates from 4.03 percentage points to 3.02 percentage points.

In the case of SC girls, the transition rate has increased from 80 percent in 2004-05 to 83 percent in 2005-06 leaving a gender gap of 3 percentage points. The picture is comparable in the case of ST girls for whom the transition rate has increased from 85 percent in 2004-05 to 88 percent in 2005-06 leaving a gender gap of 2 percentage points.

Constitutional And Policy Framework

The Constitution of India in Article 15(1) on right to equality, provides the basic policy framework that enshrines the vision of girls' education and the spirit in which their education is to be provided.

Until 1976, education was a State subject. Since its transfer to the Concurrent List by the 42 Constitutional Amendment in 1976, the Central Government has played a more proactive role in the sector through several centrally sponsored schemes that had a distinct bearing on promoting education for girls.

A new thrust was provided to girls' education in the National Policy on Education 1986, (as modified in 1992) which provided a holistic vision for the education of women and girls and recognized the cross cutting issues that inhibited the realization of this goal. It aims at using Education as an agent of basic change in the status of women in society.

The 86th Constitutional Amendment Act, 2002 has made elementary education a Fundamental Right for children in the age group of 6-14 years by providing that *"the State shall provide free and compulsory education to all children of the age of six to fourteen years in such manner as the State may, by law, determine"*. This has been a path breaking legislation in India, where such a major commitment to the cause of elementary education has bound governments, community based organizations and civil society into a common resolve to achieve universal elementary education.

Drawing upon the Constitution and other policy statements articulated in the years that followed, the Government of India in partnership with State Governments has designed different strategies, interventions, schemes and programmes with specific objectives that impinge on girls' education. In the second part of this essay we shall look at some of these programmes and interactions that have begun to change the face of India.

FEMALE EDUCATION

Female education is a catch-all term for a complex set of issues and debates surrounding education (primary education, secondary education, tertiary education, and health education in particular) for girls and women. It includes areas of gender equality and access to education, and its connection to the alleviation of poverty. Also involved are the issues of single-sex education and religious education in that the division of education along gender lines as well as religious teachings on education have been traditionally dominant and are still highly relevant in contemporary discussions of educating females as a global consideration.

While the feminist movement has certainly promoted the importance of the issues attached to female education the discussion is wide-ranging and by no means narrowly defined. It may include, for example, AIDS education. Universal education, meaning state-provided primary and secondary education independent of gender is not yet a global norm, even if it is assumed in most developed countries. In some Western countries, women have surpassed men at many levels of education. For example, in the United States in 2005/2006, women earned 62% of associate degrees, 58% of bachelor's degrees, 60% of master's degrees, and 50% of doctorates.

Education for women with handicaps has also improved. In 2011, Giusi Spagnolo became the first woman with Down Syndrome to graduate college in Europe (she graduated from the University of Palermo in Italy).

Improving girls' educational levels has been demonstrated to have clear impacts on the health and economic future of young women, which in turn improves the prospects of their entire community . Infant mortality rate of babies whose mothers have received primary education is half that of children whose mothers are illiterate. In the poorest countries of the world, 50% of girls do not attend secondary school. Yet, research shows that every extra year of school for girls increases their lifetime income by 15%. Improving female education, and thus the earning potential of women, improves the standard of living for their own children, as women invest more of their income in their families than men do. Yet, many barriers to education for girls remain. In some African countries, such as Burkina Faso, girls are unlikely to attend school for such basic reasons as a lack of private latrine facilities for girls.

Higher attendance rates of high schools and university education among women, particularly in developing countries, have helped them make inroads to professional careers with better-paying salaries and wages. Education increases a woman's (and her partner and the family's) level of health and health awareness. Furthering women's levels of education and advanced training also tends to lead to later ages of initiation of sexual activity and first intercourse, later age at first marriage, and later age at first childbirth, as well as an increased likelihood to remain single, have no children, or have no formal marriage and alternatively, have increasing levels of long-term partnerships. It can lead to higher rates of barrier and chemical contraceptive use (and a lower level of sexually transmitted infections among women and their partners and children), and can increase the level of resources available to women who divorce or are in a situation of domestic violence. It has been shown, in addition, to increase women's communication with their partners and their employers, and to improve rates of civic participation such as voting or the holding of office.

Chinese history

Along with the custom of footbinding among Chinese women that lasted through the end of the 19th century, it was recognized that a woman's virtue lay with her lack of knowledge. As a result, female education was not considered to be worthy of attention. With the arrival of numerous Christian missionaries from Britain and the US to China in the 19th century and some of them being involved in the starting of schools for women, female education started to receive some attention.

Due to the social custom that men and women should not be near one another, the women of China were reluctant to be treated by male doctors of Western medicine.This resulted in a tremendous need for women in Western medicine in China.Thus, female medical missionary, Dr.Mary H. Fulton (1854-1927), was sent by the Foreign Missions Board of the Presbyterian Church (USA)to found the first medical college for women in China. Known as the Hackett Medical College for Women, this College was located in Guangzhou, China, and was enabled by a large donation from Mr. Edward A.K. Hackett (1851-1916) of Indiana, United States.

The College was dedicated in 1902 and offered a four-year curriculum. By 1915, there were more than 60 students, mostly in residence. Most students became Christians, due to the influence of Dr. Fulton. The College was officially recognized, with its diplomas marked with the official stamp of the Guangdong provincial government. The College was aimed at the spreading of Christianity and modern medicine and the elevation of Chinese women's social status. The David Gregg Hospital for Women and Children (also known as Yuji Hospitalwas affiliated with this College. The graduates of this College included Lee Sun Chau, 1890-1979, alumna of (Belilios Public School) and WONG Yuen-hing, both of whom graduated in the late 1910s and then practiced medicine in the hospitals in Guangdong province.

Education after the establishment of the People's Republic of China

Between year 1931 and year 1945, the percent of uneducated women is over 90% and most of the women who got educated were in elementary level. In 1950s, after the establishment of People Republic China, the government started a civilization project. It enabled large amounts of uneducated women to learn basic writing and calculation. This project raised the proportion of educated women. It was promoted not only in cities but also in rural area. Villages had their own elementary schools. Instead of only taking care of children and chores at home, middle-aged women had chances to learn writing and reading in local schools.

In 1980s, Chinese central government passed a new education law, which required local governments to promote 9-year obligation education nationwide The new education law guaranteed education rights until middle school. Before 1960s, female enrollment in elementary school was 20%. 20 years after publishment of education law, in the year 1995, this percentage had increased to 98.2%. By 2003, proportion of female who dropped from middle school decreased to 2.49%.

According to the fifth national census in 2000, the average education length of females is up to 7.4 years. This digit increases from 7.0 years to 7.4 years in 3 years. However, the female education duration is still 0.8 year less than male's duration. This gap in higher-level of education is larger in rural areas.In the countryside, parents tend to use their limited resources for sons because they believe sons have abilities to bring more back and their contributions to family in the future are more significant than daughters. In an investigation, parents are 21.9% more likely to stop financing girls' education if they come into financial problems and family issues. Boys are provided with more opportunities for further studying, especially after middle school. This difference became more evident in the universities.

When time comes into the 21st century, university education is becoming more prevalent.The total enrollment goes up. Compare to the year of 1977, which is the first year when college entrance examination was recovered, the admission rate increased from 4.8% to 74.86%. Since the general admission has largely risen, more students got into universities. Although women are assumed to own the same rights of general education, they are forced to do better in the Chinese college entrance examination(Gaokao) than males. Girls need to achieve higher grades than male students in order to get into the same level university. It is an invisible ceiling for Chinese female, especially in the top universities. It is not a public rule but a mainstream consensus among most of Chinese university admission offices. According to a telephone interview with an officer, who declined to give her name, at the

Teaching Office at the China University of Political Science and Law, "female students must account for less than 15 percent of students because of the nature of their future career."

Islamic history

Women in Islam played an important role in the foundations of many Islamic educational institutions, such as Fatima al-Fihri's founding of the University of Al Karaouine in 859. This continued through to the Ayyubid dynasty in the 12th and 13th centuries, when 160 mosques (places of worship) and madrasahs (places of education) were established in Damascus, 26 of which were funded by women through the Waqf (charitable trust or trust law) system. Half of all the royal patrons for these institutions were also women.

According to the Sunni scholar Ibn Asakir, in the 12th century, there were opportunities for female education in the mediaeval Islamic world. Asakir wrote that women should study, earn *ijazahs*(academic degrees), and qualify as scholars and teachers. This was especially the case for learned and scholarly families, who wanted to ensure the highest possible education for both their sons and daughters. Ibn Asakir himself had studied under 80 different female teachers in his time. According to a hadith attributed to Muhammad, he praised the women of Medina because of their desire for religious knowledge.

"How splendid were the women of the Ansar (Islam) — *ansar; shame did not prevent them from becoming learned in the faith."*

While it was unusual for females to enroll as students in formal classes, it was common for women to attend informal lectures and study sessions at mosques, madrasahs, and other public places. While there were no legal restrictions on female education, some men, such as Muhammad ibn al-Hajj (d. 1336), did not approve of this practice and were appalled at the behaviour of some women who informally audited lectures in his time.

While women accounted for no more than one percent of Islamic scholars prior to the 12th century, there was a large increase of female scholars after this. In the 15th century, al-Sakhawi devoted an entire volume of his 12-volume biographical dictionary *al-aw¾ al-lâmi»* to female scholars, giving information on 1,075 of them.

More recently, the scholar Mohammad Akram Nadwi, currently a researcher from the Oxford Centre for Islamic Studies, has written 40 volumes on the mu%addithât (the women scholars of %adîth), and found at least 8,000 of them.

Women education in the Islamic Republic of Iran

After year of 1979

Since the 1979 revolution, Iran was under control of Islamic rules, the progress of female education was affected by Islamic monarchy. Women are forced to wear veiling and are prevented from going to the same school as male students. Female students have to learn different versions of textbooks, which are special editions only for female students. Unmarried women are ineligible for financial aid if they attempt to study abroad. Throughout the past 30 years, the issue of female education has been constantly under debate. Iranian women do have desires and abilities to pursue further education. An Iranian high school student can earn a diploma after studying 3 years. If students aim to enter colleges, they will stay in the high schools for the fourth year study, which has very intense study. According to researches, 42% of female students choose to have fourth year in the high school but only 28% of male students choose to study in order to enter university. Moreover, women have a much higher probability than men to pass college entrance exams. Islamic female are in need of achieving higher education and truth proved that their abilities are enough for getting higher education. The education opportunities for female need more national attention and less regulations.

During 1978 and 1979, the proportion of women who participated in universities as students or faculties was rather low. 31% of students admitted to universities were women. For faculty gender composition, there are 14% female. This situation has changed with time passing by. University enrollment was decreased under the influence of Iranian Cultural Revolution. The general enrollment population declined during that time. After the culture revolution, the amount of enrollment was going up. The increase in the number of university students is accompanied with an increase in female rate. Islamic higher education contains 5 levels.

The 5 levels are associate, bachelor's, master's, professional doctorate and specialized doctorate. Before the revolution, the gender gap is obvious in master level and specialized doctorate, which are only 20% and 27%. It has changed after 30 years. In 2007, the female percent in master's degree rose up to 43% and for specialized doctorate degree, this data rose up to 33%.

Female rate has not only increased in the students but also in faculty. 20 years ago, only 6% of all professors and 8% of all associated professors were women. Now 8% of all professors and 17% of all associated professors are female.

European history

Ancient Rome

In ancient Rome, upperclass women seem to have been well-educated, some highly so, and were sometimes praised by male historians of the time for their learning and cultivation. Cornelia Metella, for instance, was distinguished for her knowledge of geometry, literature, music, and philosophy. In the wall paintings of Pompeii, women are more likely than men to be pictured with writing implements. Some women had sufficient knowledge of Roman the law and oratorical training to conduct court cases on their own behalf, or on behalf of others. Among occupations that required education, women could be scribes and secretaries, calligraphers, and artists. Some and perhaps many Roman girls went to a ludus (ancient Rome) | public primary school. Boys and girls were educated either together or with similar methods and curriculum. One passage inLivy's history assumes that the daughter of a centurion would be in school; the social rank of a centurion was typically equivalent to modern perceptions of the "middle class". Girls as well as boys participated in public religious festivals, and sang advanced choral compositions that would require formal musical training.

Medieval period

Medieval education for females was typically tied to a convent. Research has uncovered that several early women educators were in charge of schools for girls:

St. Ita of Ireland - died 570 AD. Founder and teacher of a co-ed school for girls and boys at her monastery of Cell Ide. Several important saints studied under her, including St. Brendan the Navigator.

Caesaria the Younger - died 550 AD. Successor to the sister of St. Caesarius and abbess of the convent he founded for her nuns, Caesaria the Younger continued the teaching of over a hundred women at the convent and aided in the copying and preservation of books.

St. Hilda of Whitby - died 680 AD. Founder of the co-ed monastery of Whitby (men and women lived in separate houses), she established a center of education in her monastery similar to what was founded by the Frankish nuns. According to the Venerable Bede, "Her prudence was so great, that not only meaner men in their need, but sometimes even kings and princes, sought and received her counsel."

St. Bertilla - died c. 700 AD. Queen Bathild requested her services for the convent she had founded at Chelle. Her pupils founded convents in other parts of western Europe, including Saxony.

St. Leoba - died 782 AD. St. Boniface requested her presence on his mission to the Germans and while there she founded an influential convent and school.

St. Bede the Venerable reports that noble-women were often sent to these schools for girls even if they did not intend to pursue the religious life, and St. Aldhelm praised their curriculum for including grammar, poetry, and Scriptural study.

The biography of Sts. Herlinda and Renilda also demonstrates that women in these convent schools could be trained in art and music.

During the reign of Emperor Charlemagne, he had his wife and daughters educated in the liberal arts at the Palace Academy of Aachen,for which he is praised in the Vita Karolini Magni. There is evidence that other nobles had their daughters educated at the Palace Academy as well.

In line with this, authors such as Vincent of Beauvais indicate that the daughters of the nobility were widely given to education so that they could live up to their social position to come.

Early modern period, humanist attitudes

In early modern Europe, the question of female education had become a commonplace one, in other words a literary topos for discussion. Around 1405 Leonardo Bruni wrote *De studies et letteris,* addressed to Baptista di Montefeltro, the daughter of Antonio II da Montefeltro,Duke of Urbino; it commends the study of Latin, but warns against arithmetic, geometry, astrology and rhetoric. In discussing the classical scholar Isotta Nogarola, however, Lisa Jardine notes that (in the middle of the 15th century), *'Cultivation' is in order for a noblewoman; formal competence is positively unbecoming.* Christine de Pisan's *Livre des Trois Vertus* is contemporary with Bruni's book, and *sets down the things which a lady or baroness living on her estates ought to be able to do.*

In his 1516 book *Utopia,* Thomas More advocated for women to have the right to education.

Erasmus wrote at length about education in *De pueris instituendis* (1529, written two decades before); not mostly concerned with female education, in this work he does mention with approbation the trouble Thomas More took with teaching his whole family. Catherine of Aragon "had been born and reared in one of the most brilliant and enlightened of Europen courts, where the cultural equality of men and women was normal". By her influence, she made education for English women both popular and fashionable. In 1523, Juan Luis Vives, a follower of Erasmus, wrote in Latin his *De institutione feminae Christianae.* This work was commissioned by Catherine, who had charge of the education of her daughter for the future Queen Mary I of England; in translation it appeared as *Education of a Christian Woman.* It is in line with traditional didactic literature, taking a strongly religious direction. It also placed a strong emphasis on Latin literature.Also Comenius was an advocate of formal education for women. In fact his emphasis was on a type of universal education making no distinction between humans; with an important component allowed to parental input, he advocated in his *Pampaedia* schooling rather than other forms of tutoring, for all.

The Reformation prompted the establishment of compulsory education for boys and girls. Most important was Martin Luther's text 'An die Ratsherren aller Städte deutschen Landes,' (1524) with the call for establishing schools. Especially the Protestant South-West of theHoly Roman Empire of the German Nation with cities like Strassburg became pioneers in educational questions. Under the influence of Strasbourg in 1592 the German Duchy Pfalz-Zweibrücken became the first territory of the world with compulsory education for girls and boys.

Elizabeth I of England had a strong humanist education, and was praised by her tutor Roger Ascham. She fits the pattern of education for leadership, rather than for the generality of women. When Johannes Sturm published Latin correspondence with Ascham centred on the achievements in humanist study of Elizabeth and other high-ranking English persons, in Konrad Heresbach's *De laudibus Graecarum literarum oratio* (1551), the emphasis was on the nobility of those tackling the classics, rather than gender.

So schooling for girls was not always rare.

Modern period

The issue of female education in the large, as emancipatory and rational, is broached seriously inthe Enlightenment. Mary Wollstonecraft, who worked as a teacher, governess, and school-owner, wrote of it in those terms. Her first book was *Thoughts on the Education of Daughters,* years before the publication of *A Vindication of the Rights of Woman.*

The Commission of National Education in the Polish-Lithuanian Commonwealth, founded in 1777, considered the first Ministry of Education in history, was a central, autonomous body responsible for nationwide, secular and coeducational training. In the late 19th century, in what was then the Russian province of Poland, in response to the lack of higher training for women, the so-called Flying University was organized, where women were taught covertly by Polish scholars and academics. Its most famous student was Maria Sk³odowska-Curie, better known as Marie

Curie, who went on to win two Nobel Prizes. Much education was channelled through religious establishments. Not all of these educated women only for marriage and motherhood; for example, Quaker views on women had allowed much equality from the foundation of the denomination in the mid-17th century. The abolitionist William Allen and his wife Grizell Hoare set up the Newington Academy for Girls in 1824, teaching an unusually wide range of subjects from languages to sciences. The first state-financed higher education institution for women in Europe, was established by Catherine II of Russia

Actual progress in institutional terms, for secular education of women, began in the West in the 19th century, with the founding of colleges offering single-sex education to young women. These appeared in the middle of the century. *The Princess: A Medley*, a narrative poem by Alfred Lord Tennyson, is a satire of women's education, still a controversial subject in 1848, when Queen's College first opened in London.

Emily Davies campaigned for women's education in the 1860s, and founded Girton College in 1869, as did Anne Clough found Newnham Collegein 1875. Progress was gradual, and often depended on individual efforts - for example, those of Frances Lupton, which led to the founding of the Leeds Girls' High School in 1876. W. S. Gilbert parodied Tennyson's poem and treated the themes of women's higher education andfeminism in general with *The Princess* in (1870) and *Princess Ida* in 1883.

Once women began to graduate from institutions of higher education, there steadily developed also a stronger academic stream of schooling, and the teacher training of women in larger numbers, principally to provide primary education. Women's access to traditionally all-male institutions took several generations to become complete.

Educational reform

The interrelated themes of barriers to education and employment continued to form the backbone of feminist thought in the 19th century, as described, for instance by Harriet Martineau in her 1859 article "Female Industry" in the *Edinburgh Journal*.

Despite the changes in the economy, the position of women in society had not greatly improved and unlike Frances Power Cobbe, Martineau did not support the emerging call for the vote for practical reasons.

Slowly the efforts of women like Emily Davies and the Langham group (under Barbara Leigh Smith Bodichon) started to make inroads. Queen's College (1848) and Bedford College (1849) in London started to offer some education to women, and by 1862 Davies was establishing a committee to persuade the universities to allow women to sit for the recently established (1858) Cambridge Local Examinations, with partial success (1865). A year later she published *The Higher Education of Women.* She and Bodichon founded the first higher educational institution for women, with five students, which became Girton College, Cambridge in 1873, followed by Lady Margaret Hall at Oxford in 1879. Bedford had started awarding degrees the previous year. Despite these measurable advances, few could take advantage of them and life for women students was very difficult.

As part of the continuing dialogue between British and American feminists, Elizabeth Blackwell, the first woman in the US to graduate in medicine (1849), lectured in Britain with Langham support. They also supported Elizabeth Garrett'sattempts to assail the walls of British medical education against strong opposition; she eventually took her degree in France. Garrett's successful campaign to run for office on the London School Board in 1870 is another example of how a small band of determined women were starting to reach positions of influence at the level of local government and public bodies.

Africa

Christian missionaries in the 19th century opened modern educational methods, but they usually focused on boys. After early experiments they settled on promoting ideology of domestic femininity imparted through girls' schooling. In South Africa after 1820, male Scottish missionaries decided that only the most basic education was necessary to prepare native women for the propagation of Christianity within the home. They prevented female teachers from operating in the Scottish mission's territory. They delayed the establishment of a Girls' Department at Lovedale Institution. Finally new leadership arrived who had a broader vision of uplifting native women so they could promote Christianity and Western gender codes.

Muslims from India who came to East Africa in the late 19th century brought along a highly restrictive policy against schooling for their girls.

As of 2015, Priscilla Sitienei is attending elementary school in Kenya at age 92; if confirmed by the Guinness World Records, she would be the oldest student in elementary school.

India

Ancient Vedic age (~1000 BC)

The history of female education in India has its roots in ancient Vedic age.

"The home has, verily, its foundation in the wife" - The Rig Veda

During the Vedic age, more than 3,000 years ago, women were assigned a high place in society. They shared an equal standing with their men folk and enjoyed a kind of liberty that actually had societal sanctions. The ancient Hindu philosophical concept of 'shakti', the feminine principle of energy, was also a product of this age. This took the form of worship of the female idols or goddesses. In India even today people worship Goddess "Saraswati" as the Goddess of education. Vedic literature praises the birth of a scholarly daughter in these words: "A girl also should be brought up and educated with great effort and care." (Mahanirvana Tantra); and "All forms of knowledge are aspects of Thee; and all women throughout the world are Thy forms." (Devi Mahatmya).

Women, who so desired, could undergo the sacred thread ceremony or 'Upanayana' (a sacrament to pursue Vedic studies), which is only meant for males even to this day. The mention of female scholars and sages of the Vedic age like Vac, Ambhrni, Romasa, Gargi, Khona in the Vedic lore corroborates this view.

These highly intelligent and greatly learned women, who chose the path of Vedic studies, were called 'brahmavadinis', and women who opted out of education for married life were called 'sadyovadhus'. Co-education seems to have existed in this period and both the sexes got equal attention from the teacher. Moreover, ladies from the Kshatriya caste received martial arts courses and arms training

Women of the Vedic period (circa 1500-1200 BCE), were epitomes of intellectual and spiritual attainments. The Vedas have volumes to say about these women, who both complemented and supplemented their male partners. When it comes to talking about significant female figures of the Vedic period, four names - Ghosha, Lopamudra, Sulabha Maitreyi, and Gargi - come to mind.

Ghosha

Vedic wisdom is encapsulated in myriad hymns and 27 women-seers emerge from them. But most of them are mere abstractions except for a few, such as Ghosha, who has a definite human form. Granddaughter of Dirghatamas and daughter of Kakshivat, both composers of hymns in praise of Ashwins, Ghosha has two entire hymns of the tenth book, each containing 14 verses, assigned to her name.

The first eulogizes the Ashwins, the heavenly twins who are also physicians; the second is a personal wish expressing her intimate feelings and desires for married life. Ghosha suffered from an incurable disfiguring disease, probably leprosy, and remained a spinster at her father's house. Her implorations with the Ashwins, and the devotion of her forefathers towards them made them cure her disease and allow her to experience wedded bliss.

Lopamudra

The Rig Veda ('Royal Knowledge') has long conversations between the sage Agasthya and his wife Lopamudra that testifies to the great intelligence and goodness of the latter. As the legend goes, Lopamudra was created by sage Agasthya and was given as a daughter to the King of Vidarbha. The royal couple gave her the best possible education and brought her up amidst luxury.

When she attained a marriageable age, Agasthya, the sage who was under vows of celibacy and poverty, wanted to own her. Lopa agreed to marry him, and left her palace for Agasthya's hermitage.

After serving her husband faithfully for a long period, Lopa grew tired of his austere practices. She wrote a hymn of two stanzas making an impassioned plea for his attention and love. Soon afterwards, the sage realized his duties towards his wife and performed both his domestic and ascetic life with equal zeal, reaching a wholeness of spiritual and physical powers. A son was born to them. He was named Dridhasyu, who later became a great poet.

Maitreyi

The Rig Veda contains about one thousand hymns, of which about 10 are accredited to Maitreyi, the woman seer and philosopher. She contributed towards the enhancement of her sage-husband Yajnavalkya's personality and the flowering of his spiritual thoughts. Yajnavalkya had two wives Maitreyi and Katyayani.

While Maitreyi was well versed in the Hindu scriptures and was a 'brahmavadini', Katyayani was an ordinary woman. One day the sage decided to make a settlement of his worldly possessions between his two wives and renounce the world by taking up ascetic vows. He asked his wives their wishes. The learned Maitreyi asked her husband if all the wealth in the world would make her immortal. The sage replied that wealth could only make one rich, nothing else. She then asked for the wealth of immortality. Yajnavalkya was happy to hear this, and imparted Maitreyi the doctrine of the soul and his knowledge of attaining immortality.

Gargi

Gargi, the Vedic prophetess and daughter of sage Vachaknu, composed several hymns that questioned the origin of all existence. When King Janak of Videha organized a 'brahmayajna', a philosophic congress centered around the fire sacrament, Gargi was one of the eminent participants. She challenged the sage Yajnavalkya with a volley of perturbing questions on the soul or 'atman' that confounded the learned man who had till then silenced many an eminent scholar. Her question - "The layer that is above the sky and below the earth, which is described as being situated between the earth and the sky and which is indicated as the symbol of the past, present and future, where is that situated?" - bamboozled even the great Vedic men of letters.

British India

Women's employment and education was acknowledged in 1854 by the East India Company's Programme: Wood's Dispatch. Slowly, after that, there was progress in female education, but it initially tended to be focused on the primary school level and was related to the richer sections of society. The overall literacy rate for women increased from 0.2% in 1882 to 6% in 1947.

In western India Jyotiba Phule and his wife Savitribai became pioneers of female education when they started a school for girls in 1848 in Pune.

In 1878, the University of Calcutta became one of the first universities to admit female graduates to its degree programmes, before any of the British universities had later done the same. This point was raised during the Ilbert Bill controversy in 1883, when it was being considered whether Indian judges should be given the right to judge British offenders. The role of women featured prominently in the controversy, where English women who opposed the bill argued that Bengali women, whom they stereotyped as "ignorant" and neglected by their men and that Indian men should therefore not be given the right to judge cases involving English women. Bengali women who supported the bill responded by claiming that they were more educated than the English women opposed to the bill and pointed out that more Indian women had degrees than British women did at the time.

Independent India

After India attained independence in 1947, the University Education Commission was created to recommend suggestions to improve the quality of education. However, their report spoke against female education, referring to it as: "Women's present education is entirely irrelevant to the life they have to lead. It is not only a waste but often a definite disability."

However, the fact that the female literacy rate was at 8.9% post-Independence could not be ignored. Thus, in 1958, a national committee on women's education was appointed by the government, and most of its recommendations were accepted. The crux of its recommendations were to bring female education on the same footing as offered for boys.

Soon afterward, committees were created that talked about equality between men and women in the field of education. For example, one committee on differentiation of curricula for boys and girls (1959) recommended equality and a common curricula at various stages of their learning.

Further efforts were made to expand the education system, and the Education Commission was set up in 1964, which largely talked about female education, which recommended a national policy to be developed by the government. This occurred in 1968, providing increased emphasis on female education.

Current policies

Before and after Independence, India has been taking active steps towards women's status and education. The 86th Constitutional Amendment Act, 2002, has been a path breaking step towards the growth of education, especially for females. According to this act, elementary education is a fundamental right for children between the ages of 6 and 14. The government has undertaken to provide this education free of cost and make it compulsory for those in that age group. This undertaking is more widely known as Sarva Shiksha Abhiyan (SSA).

Since then, the SSA has come up with many schemes for inclusive as well as exclusive growth of Indian education as a whole, including schemes to help foster the growth of female education. The major schemes are the following:

- Mahila Samakhya Programme: This programme was launched in 1988 as a result of the New Education Policy

(1968). It was created for the empowerment of women from rural areas especially socially and economically marginalized groups. When the SSA was formed, it initially set up a committee to look into this programme, how it was working and recommend new changes that could be made.

- Kasturba Gandhi Balika Vidyalaya Scheme(KGBV): This scheme was launched in July, 2004, to provide education to girls at primary level. It is primarily for the underprivileged and rural areas where literacy level for females is very low. The schools that were set up have 100% reservation: 75% for backward class and 25% for BPL (below Poverty line) females.
- National Programme for Education of Girls at Elementary Level (NPEGEL): This programme was launched in July, 2003. It was an incentive to reach out to the girls who the SSA was not able to reach through other schemes. The SSA called out to the "hardest to reach girls". This scheme has covered 24 states in India. Under the NPEGEL, "model schools" have been set up to provide better opportunities to girls.

One notable success came in 2013, when the first two girls ever scored in the top 10 ranks of the entrance exam to the Indian Institutes of Technology (IITs). Sibbala Leena Madhuri ranked eighth, and Aditi Laddha ranked sixth.

Raising awareness

The Canadian start-up Decode Global has developed the mobile game Get Water!, a game for social change focusing on the water scarcity in India and the effect it has on girls' education, especially in slums and rural areas. In areas with no ready access to water, girls are often pulled out of school to collect water for their families.

Catholic tradition

In the Roman Catholic tradition, concern for female education has expressed itself from the days of the Catechetical School of Alexandria, which in the 200s AD had courses for both men and women. Later Church writers such as St. Ambrose, St. Augustine, and St. Jeromeall left letters of instruction for women in convents that they either founded or supported. In the medieval ages, several religious instituteswere established with ministries addressing women's education. For medieval examples of convent schools, which are one form of such institutions, see the examples at the section on the medieval period. In the early modern period, this tradition was continued with theUrsulines (1535) and the Religious of the Sacred Heart of Mary (1849). Contemporary convent schools are usually not restricted to Catholic pupils. Students in contemporary convent education may be boys (particularly in India).

THE FUTURE OF WOMEN'S EDUCATION

Present Conditions in Women's Education-In our visits to many colleges we have had numerous opportunities to inquire into and to observe the conditions and workings of women's education. It is very clear that there are certain steps which urgently need to be, taken to make the conditions of women's education more tolerable.

There are few truly co-educational colleges in our country. Rather, there are men,s colleges to which women have been admitted as students, which is a very different matter. Quite frequently in "Co- educational" colleges nearly all the amenities are for men, and women are little more than tolerated. Often sanitary facilities for women are totally inadequate, and sometimes wholly lacking. Recreation space and facilities for women similarly are inadequateor lacking. One of the most frequent suggestions made to us was that where women and men attend colleges that a, physical directress for women be provided. In many co-educational colleges women have little or no share, in college life Women's hostels usually accommodate but few women, and Sometimes none at all. According to the comments received, in one city where there are few or no hostels some women students must, leave home at 5 A.M. in order to attend classes, and not provisions for refreshments are provided, although the students do not finish their work until mid-afternoon. The commission received comments to the effect that the attitudes of men students left, much to be desired. Other weaknesses of "co-educational" colleges reported to our commission are that there are too few women teachers, and that examinations are a severe nervous strain to women.

Suggestions for Improvement-Among the many suggestions received are that women in seclusion should be allowed to appear for examinations; that special consideration be given to the status and needs of women; that in the employment of women staff members, there should be equal pay for equal work as compared with men. We were informed that while a considerable number of women take medical courses, relatively few actually practise medicine. Since medical education is very expensive, and student enrolment in medical schools necessarily small, to train a person who will not practise is a social loss. To the extent that is the case, women's interests might well be redirected to nursing, medical laboratory technology, dietetics, and other callings where the period of training and the expenses are less. Social taboos are a large, element in retarding such redirection of interest. Here as elswehere, a democratic spirit does not necessary follow a democratic constitutions. Such redirec- tion of interest should be a matter of counsel and advice, rather than of compulsion. The medical profession should remain open to women.

Co-education-The question of the wisdom of co-education was frequently raised, and the most divergent opinions were expressed. There seems to be a definite preponderance of opinion that from the thirteenth or fourteenth year of age until about the eighteenth, separate schools for boys and girls are desirable. Whether this opinion 'is chiefly based on custom or upon experience is not wholly clear.

One of India's prominent educators states "The modern trend is for equality of opportunity for women in all spheres, and it cannot be arrested. There should be no distinctions of any kind of women from men, after the matriculation stage". On the other hand many, probably a majority of those who Commented, favour separate colleges for women when that is feasible, though not to the extent of denying women educational opportunity by excluding them from existing colleges organised Primarily for men.

Some of the arguments given are that a women cannot develop her personality in a men's college: that here is no need for women to undergo the nervous strain of examinations; that woman's education should be more in keeping with the temperament and needs of Women as wives and mothers: and that overcrowding is more serious for women than for men. "A pleasing feature of colleges for women has been the intimate relations of students and teachers." Some of these arguments have greater weight in the absence of truly coeducational colleges where the needs of men and women would be given equal weight in designing the programme.

As the age of entry to degree colleges would, on our recommendation, be approximately eighteen, college education may be co-educational, as it is present in many medical colleges. Separate institutions at this level would demand unjustified increase in expense. To maintain separate institutions for men and women side by side, duplicating equipment, even when it is very inadequate, would be an undue tax upon limited financial resources. Separate women's colleges commonly have poorer buildings, poorer equipment, and less able teachers. So far as possible co-educational institutions should be encouraged at the degree level. Appraisals of Women's Education-The results of women's education under existing conditions have not been entirely satisfactory. The principal of a college wrote: "women's present education is entirely irrelevant to the life they have to lead. It is not only a waste, but often a definite disability." Another wrote, "The present system of women's education, based as it is upon man's needs, does not in any way make them fit for coping with the practical problems of daily life. Their education should give them a practical bias, especially from the point of view of families, for making them good mothers, teachers, doctors and nurses".

One experienced woman educator wrote to the Commission "The modern educated Indian woman is neither happy nor contented nor socially useful. She is a misfit in life. She is highly suppressed, an needs opportunities for self-expression, the new education must provide this opportunity." To some extent this maladjustment is the price of pioneering. The educated woman is ahead of her time. She is lonely and "out of place" while creating a new social atmosphere in which her daughter or grand daughter can be natural and at home. But to some extent her discontent is due to her effort, not only to be equal to men, but to be like them in all her interests and activities.

One educator wrote: "It is too late in the day to suggest that women should not have the same courses as men. The remaining question is, what additional opportunities shall be provided?" It is the duty of those in charge of women's education to face these problems, and to design education for women which will enable them to have full and adequate lives. One educator wrote: "There has been a no planning of women's education. It has just happened".

6

Child Abuse in India

One of the biggest social stigmas attached to a society is that of child abuse. A child can be abused physically, sexually or mentally. It can be in the form of injury, neglect or negligent treatment, blaming, forced sexual stimulation and activity, incest exploitation and sexual abuse. Child abuse can take place in homes, schools, orphanages, residential care facilities, on the streets, in the workplace, in prisons and in places of detention. Violence in any form has a very deep impact on the overall development of the child. Child abuse results in actual or potential harm to the child's health, survival, development and dignity.

53% of children in India face some form of child sexual abuse. According to the National Crime Records Bureau, the cases of rape and murder of children increase every year. The growing complexities of life and the changed social economic conditions have exposed the children to new and different forms of abuse. But the sad state of the affairs is that such heinous acts are reported less. It has such a psychological impact on the mind of the child that he seldom gathers the courage to speak about the act being committed against him. If even if he confides the fact with someone, the social factors let the fact being dumped under the fear of family reputation and other related issues. In fact child abuse is a violation of the basic human rights of a child.

What Is Child Abuse?

As per the definition given by UNICEF, violence can be physical and mental abuse and injury, neglect or negligent treatment, exploitation and sexual abuse. Violence may take place in homes, schools, orphanages, residential care facilities, on the streets, in the workplace, in prisons and in places of detention. Such violence can affect the normal development of a child impairing their mental, physical and social being. In extreme cases abuse of a child can result in death.

Child abuse has many forms: physical, emotional, sexual, neglect, and exploitation. Any of these that are potentially or actually harmful to a child's health, survival, dignity and development are abuse.

Physical Abuse

Physical abuse is the inflicting of physical injury upon a child. This may include burning, hitting, punching, shaking, kicking, beating or otherwise harming a child. The parent or caretaker may not have intended to hurt the child. It may, however, be the result of over-discipline or physical punishment that is inappropriate to the child's age.

Sexual Abuse

Sexual abuse is inappropriate sexual behaviour with a child. It includes fondling a child's genitals, making the child fondle the adult's genitals, intercourse, incest, rape, sodomy, exhibitionism and sexual exploitation. To be considered 'child abuse', these acts have to be committed by a person responsible for the care of a child (for example a baby-sitter, a parent, or a daycare provider), or related to the child. If a stranger commits these acts, it would be considered sexual assault and handled solely by the police and criminal courts.

Emotional Abuse

Emotional abuse is also known as verbal abuse, mental abuse, and psychological maltreatment. It includes acts or the failures to act by parents or caretakers that have caused or could cause, serious behavioral, cognitive, emotional, or mental trauma. This can include parents/caretakers using extreme and/or bizarre forms of punishment, such as confinement in a closet or dark room or being tied to a chair for long periods of time or threatening or terrorizing a child. Less severe acts, but no less damaging, are belittling or rejecting treatment, using derogatory terms to describe the child, habitual tendency to blame the child or make him/her a scapegoat.

Neglect

It is the failure to provide for the child's basic needs. Neglect can be physical, educational, or emotional. Physical neglect can include not providing adequate food or clothing, appropriate medical care, supervision, or proper weather protection (heat or cold). It may include abandonment. Educational neglect includes failure to provide appropriate schooling or special educational needs, allowing excessive ancestries. Psychological neglect includes the lack of any emotional support and love, never attending to the child, substance abuse including allowing the child to participate in drug and alcohol use.

PHYSICAL ABUSE

The World Health Organization defines 'physical abuse' of a child as an incident resulting in actual or potential physical harm from an interaction or lack of interaction, which is reasonably within the control of a parent or person in a position of responsibility, power, or trust.

There may be single or repeated incidents. The Indian society demands the children to be obedient to their parents. Any form of disobedience leads to anguish amongst the parents as to the misbehavior of the child which often leads to the reprimanding the child. Parents often resort to physical beating of the child to discipline the child. Not only does the parents resort to physical abuse of the child but it more common in schools and workplaces where the children are physically maltreated for their wrongs. Corporal punishment to a child whether it is at school, home or at workplace amounts to violation of the human rights of the child. It violates the right of the child to live with dignity and freedom from violence, their right to be loved and cared for and their right to be nurtured with respect. Physical abuse creates a feeling of resentment and harshness in the child.

Sexual Abuse

As defined by the World Health Organization, child sexual abuse is the involvement of a child in sexual activity that he or she does not fully comprehend, is unable to give informed consent to, or that violates the laws or social taboos of society. Child sexual abuse is evidenced by this activity between a child and an adult or another child who by age or development is in a relationship of responsibility, trust or power, the activity being intended to gratify or satisfy the needs of the other person. This may include but is not limited to:

- The inducement or coercion of a child to engage in any unlawful activity
- The exploitative use of a child in prostitution or other unlawful sexual practices
- The exploitative use of children in pornographic performances and materials.

53% of children in India face some form of child sexual abuse. Children who report having been sexually assaulted is 6% and the cases where the abuser was in a relationship of trust with the child is 50%. Home is the place where the child is the safest but now days the scenario has changed. In most of the cases of sexual abuse some close relative is the perpetrator o the crime. Due to fear the child does not complain about the incident. Such matters as secretly dumped inside the walls of the house to protect the reputation of the family. Children working as domestic labour or help in hotels and restaurants or any other place of work are susceptible to sexual abuse. Moreover the abandoned children are also easy victims of the crime. A number of children ago missing ever year and are forced to enter prostitution and exposed to other forms of sexual abuse. Children nowhere are safe from the heinous act of sexual abuse. Poverty, age, gender, caste, lack of safe spaces, lack of schools, lack of proper institutional care for children without functional families, etc make the child prone to sexual abuse. As compared to girls, the boys are also at an equal risk of sexual abuse. Sexual abuse affects the social, mental and physical growth and outlook of the child.

Emotional Abuse

The World Health Organization (WHO) has defined emotional abuse to include the failure to provide a developmentally appropriate, supportive environment, including the availability of a primary attachment figure, so that the child can develop a stable and full range of emotional and social competencies commensurate with her or his personal potentials and in the context of the society in which the child dwells.

There may also be acts towards the child that cause or have a high probability of causing harm to the child's health or physical, mental, spiritual, moral or social development.

These acts must be reasonably within the control of the parent or person in a relationship of responsibility, trust or power. Acts include restriction of movement, patterns of belittling, and denigrating, scapegoating, threatening, scaring, discriminating, ridiculing or other non-physical forms of hostile or rejecting treatment.

Examples of these acts are restricting movement, threatening, scaring, discriminating, ridiculing, belittling, etc. In India a rising concern is the pressure children feel to perform well in school and college examinations, which can be seen as a form of emotional stress and abuse. The children who had undergone emotional are more prone to depression, estrangement, anxiety, low self-esteem, inappropriate or troubled relationships, or a lack of empathy.

Neglect

Neglect or negligent treatment is purposeful omission of some or all developmental needs of the child by a caregiver with the intention of harming the child. This includes the failure of protecting the child from a harmful situation or environment when feasible. Not providing adequate food or clothing to the child, not providing adequate medical care, rejection and abandonment, failure to provide appropriate schooling, lack of emotional support and love are some forms of neglect. Our Indian society has a special affection for sons and this scenario the daughters are often neglected by the families while the sons are given preference in everything. Children who face neglect from their family and friends become quite suffer from psychological complications. It again affects their physical and mental growth and often such children turn very aggressive also.

SEXUAL ABUSE

Child sexual abuse (CSA) is a form of child abuse in which an adult or older adolescent abuses a child for sexual stimulation. Sexual abuse refers to the participation of a child in a sexual act aimed toward the physical gratification or the financial profit of the person committing the act. Forms of CSA include asking or pressuring a child to engage in sexual activities (regardless of the outcome), indecent exposure of the genitals to a child, displaying pornography to a child, actual sexual contact with a child, physical contact with the child's genitals, viewing of the child's genitalia without physical contact, or using a child to produce child pornography. Selling the sexual services of children may be viewed and treated as child abuse with services offered to the child rather than simple incarceration.

Effects of child sexual abuse on the victim(s) include guilt and self-blame, flashbacks, nightmares, insomnia, fear of things associated with the abuse (including objects, smells, places, doctor's visits, etc.), self-esteem difficulties, sexual dysfunction, chronic pain, addiction, self-injury, suicidal ideation, somatic complaints, depression, post-traumatic stress disorder, anxiety, other mental illnesses including borderline personality disorder and dissociative identity disorder, propensity to re-victimization in adulthood, bulimia nervosa, and physical injury to the child, among other problems.

Children who are the victims are also at an increased risk of sexually transmitted infections due to their immature immune systems and a high potential for mucosal tears during forced sexual contact. Sexual victimization at a young age has been correlated with several risk factors for contracting HIV including decreased knowledge of sexual topics, increased prevalence of HIV, engagement in risky sexual practices, condom avoidance, lower knowledge of safe sex practices, frequent changing of sexual partners, and more years of sexual activity.

In the United States, approximately 15% to 25% of women and 5% to 15% of men were sexually abused when they were children. Most sexual abuse offenders are acquainted with their victims; approximately 30% are relatives of the child, most often brothers, sisters, fathers, mothers, uncles or cousins; around 60% are other acquaintances such as friends of the family, babysitters, or neighbours; strangers are the offenders in approximately 10% of child sexual abuse cases. In over one-third of cases, the perpetrator is also a minor.

In 1999 the BBC reported on the RAHI Foundation's survey of sexual abuse in India, in which 76% of respondents said they had been abused as children, 40% of those stating the perpetrator was a family member.

Psychological abuse

There are multiple definitions of child psychological abuse:

- In 2013, the American Psychological Association (APA) added Child Psychological Abuse to the DSM-5, describing it as "nonaccidental verbal or symbolic acts by a child's parent or caregiver that result, or have reasonable potential to result, in significant psychological harm to the child."
- In 1995, APSAC defined it as: spurning, terrorizing, isolating, exploiting, corrupting, denying emotional responsiveness, or neglect" or "A repeated pattern of caregiver behavior or extreme incident(s) that convey to children that they are worthless, flawed, unloved, unwanted, endangered, or only of value in meeting another's needs"
- In the United States, states laws vary, but most have laws against "mental injury"
- Some have defined it as the production of psychological and social defects in the growth of a child as a result of behavior such as loud yelling, coarse and rude attitude, inattention, harsh criticism, and denigration of the child's personality. Other examples include name-calling, ridicule, degradation, destruction of personal belongings, torture

or killing of a pet, excessive criticism, inappropriate or excessive demands, withholding communication, and routine labeling or humiliation.

In 2014, the APA stated that:

- "Childhood psychological abuse [is] as harmful as sexual or physical abuse."
- "Nearly 3 million U.S. children experience some form of [psychological] maltreatment annually."
- Psychological maltreatment is "the most challenging and prevalent form of child abuse and neglect."
- "Given the prevalence of childhood psychological abuse and the severity of harm to young victims, it should be at the forefront of mental health and social service training"

In 2015, additional research confirmed these 2014 statements of the APA.

Victims of emotional abuse may react by distancing themselves from the abuser, internalizing the abusive words, or fighting back by insulting the abuser. Emotional abuse can result in abnormal or disrupted attachment development, a tendency for victims to blame themselves (self-blame) for the abuse, learned helplessness, and overly passive behavior.

Neglect

Child neglect is the failure of a parent or other person with responsibility for the child, to provide needed food, clothing, shelter, medical care, or supervision to the degree that the child's health, safety or well-being may be threatened with harm. Neglect is also a lack of attention from the people surrounding a child, and the non-provision of the relevant and adequate necessities for the child's survival, which would be a lacking in attention, love, and nurture. Some observable signs of child neglect include: the child is frequently absent from school, begs or steals food or money, lacks needed medical and dental care, is consistently dirty, or lacks sufficient clothing for the weather. The 2010 Child Maltreatment Report (NCANDS), a yearly United States federal government report based on data supplied by state Child Protective Services

(CPS) Agencies in the U.S., states, "as in prior years, neglect was the most common form of maltreatment".

Neglectful acts can be divided into six sub-categories:

- Supervisory Neglect: characterized by the absence of a parent or guardian which can lead to physical harm, sexual abuse or criminal behavior;
- Physical Neglect: characterized by the failure to provide the basic physical necessities, such as a safe and clean home;
- Medical Neglect: characterized by the lack of providing medical care;
- Emotional Neglect: characterized by a lack of nurturance, encouragement and support;
- Educational Neglect: characterized by the caregivers lack to provide an education and additional resources to actively participate in the school system; and
- Abandonment: when the parent or guardian leaves a child alone for a long period of time without a babysitter.

Neglected children may experience delays in physical and psychosocial development, possibly resulting in psychopathology and impaired neuropsychological functions including executive function, attention, processing speed, language, memory and social skills. Researchers investigating maltreated children have repeatedly found that neglected children in foster and adoptive populations manifest different emotional and behavioral reactions to regain lost or secure relationships and are frequently reported to have disorganized attachments and a need to control their environment.

Such children are not likely to view caregivers as being a source of safety, and instead typically show an increase in aggressive and hyperactive behaviors which may disrupt healthy or secure attachment with their adopted parents. These children have apparently learned to adapt to an abusive and inconsistent caregiver by becoming cautiously self-reliant, and are often described as glib, manipulative and disingenuous in their interactions with others as they move through childhood. Children who are victims of neglect have a more difficult time forming and maintaining relationships, such as romantic or friendship, later in life due to the lack of attachment they had in their earlier stages of life.

Effects

Child abuse can result in immediate adverse physical effects but it is also strongly associated with developmental problems and with many chronic physical and psychological effects, including subsequent ill-health, including higher rates of chronic conditions, high-risk health behaviors and shortened lifespan. Maltreated children may grow up to be maltreating adults. A 1991 source reported that studies indicate that 90 percent of maltreating adults were maltreated as children. Almost 7 million American infants receive child care services, such as day care, and much of that care is poor.

Emotional

Child abuse can cause a range of emotional effects. Children who are constantly ignored, shamed, terrorized or humiliated suffer at least as much, if not more, than if they are physically assaulted. According to the Joy Heart Foundation, many Childhood Development studies show that the brain development of the child is greatly influenced and responds to the experiences with families, caregivers, and the community. Abused children can grow up experiencing insecurities, low self-esteem, and lack of development. Many abused children experience ongoing difficulties with trust, social withdrawal, trouble in school, and forming relationships.

The effects of abused children can also differ when it comes to babies and young children. Babies and pre-school children who are being emotionally abused or neglected may be overly affectionate towards strangers or people they haven't known for very long.

They can lack confidence or become anxious, appear to not have a close relationship with their parent, exhibit aggressive behavior or act nasty towards other children and animals. Older children may use foul language or act in a markedly different way to other children at the same age, struggle to control strong emotions, seem isolated from their parents, lack social skills or have few, if any, friends.

Children can also experience reactive attachment disorder (RAD). RAD is defined as markedly disturbed and developmentally inappropriate social relatedness, that usually begins before the age of 5 years. RAD can present as a persistent failure to start or respond in a developmentally appropriate fashion to most social situations.

The long-term impact of emotional abuse has not been studied widely, but recent studies have begun to document its long-term consequences.

Emotional abuse has been linked to increased depression, anxiety, and difficulties in interpersonal relationships (Spertus, Wong, Halligan, & Seremetis, 2003). Victims of child abuse and neglect are more likely to commit crimes as juveniles and adults.

Domestic violence also takes its toll on children; although the child is not the one being abused, he/she witnessing the domestic violence is greatly influential as well.

Research studies conducted such as the "Longitudinal Study on the Effects of Child Abuse and Children's Exposure to Domestic Violence", show that 36.8% of children engage in felony assault compared to the 47.5% of abused/assaulted children.

Research has shown that children exposed to domestic violence increases the chances of behavioral and emotional problems (depression, anxiety, and academic problems).

Overall, emotional effects caused by child abuse and even witnessing abuse can result in long-term and short-term effects that ultimately affect a child's upbringing and development.

Physical

The immediate physical effects of abuse or neglect can be relatively minor (bruises or cuts) or severe (broken bones, hemorrhage, or even death). In some cases the physical effects are temporary; however, the pain and suffering they cause a child should not be discounted. Rib fractures may be seen with physical abuse, and if present may increase suspicion of abuse, but are found in a small minority of children with maltreatment-related injuries.

The long-term impact of child abuse and neglect on physical health and development can be:

- Shaken baby syndrome. Shaking a baby is a common form of child abuse that often results in permanent neurological damage (80% of cases) or death (30% of cases). Damage results from intracranial hypertension (increased pressure in the skull) after bleeding in the brain, damage to the spinal cord and neck, and rib or bone fractures.
- Impaired brain development. Child abuse and neglect have been shown, in some cases, to cause important regions of the brain to fail to form or grow properly, resulting in impaired development. These alterations in brain maturation have long-term consequences for cognitive, language, and academic abilities.
- Poor physical health. In addition to possible immediate adverse physical effects, household dysfunction and childhood maltreatment are strongly associated with many chronic physical and psychological effects, including subsequent ill-health in childhood, adolescence and adulthood, with higher rates of chronic conditions, high-risk health behaviors and shortened lifespan. Adults who experienced abuse or neglect during childhood are more likely to suffer from physical ailments such as allergies, arthritis, asthma, bronchitis, high blood pressure, and ulcers. There may be a higher risk of developing cancer later in life, as well as possible immune dysfunction.
- Exposure to violence during childhood is associated with shortened telomeres and with reduced telomerase activity. The increased rate of telomere length reduction correlates to a reduction in lifespan of 7 to 15 years.

THE SEXUAL ABUSE OF CHILDREN TODAY

In America, the most accurate scientific studies, based on lengthy interviews, report that 30 percent of men and 40 percent of women remember having been sexually molested during childhood---defining "molestation" as actual genital contact, not just exposure. About half of these are directly incestuous, with the family members, the other half usually being with others, but with the complicity of caretakers in at least 80 percent of the cases.

These experiences of seduction are not just pieced together from fragmentary memories, but are remembered in detail, are usually for an extended period of time and have been confirmed by follow-up reliability studies in 83 percent of the cases, so they are unlikely to have been fantasies. The seductions occurred at much earlier ages than had been previously assumed, with 81 percent occurring before puberty and an astonishing 42 percent under age 7.

As high as these molestation rates seem, however, they represent only a portion of the true rates, not only because those interviewed do not include populations that have been shown to have extremely high rates---such as criminals, prostitutes, juveniles in shelters, psychotics, etc.--but also because only conscious memories were counted, and the earliest seductions of children are almost never remembered except during psychotherapy. Adjusting statistically for what is known about these additional factors, I have concluded that the real sexual abuse rate for America is 60 percent for girls and 45 percent for boys, about half of these directly incestuous.

Other Western nations have made fewer careful studies. A recent Canadian study by Gallup of 2,000 adults has produced incidence rates almost exactly the same as those found in the United States. Latin American family sexual activity--particularly widespread pederasty as part of macho sexuality--is considered even more widespread. In England, a recent BBC "ChildWatch" program asked its female listeners--a large though admittedly biased sample--if they remembered sexual molestation, and, of the 2,530 replies analyzed, 83 percent remembered someone touching their genitals, 62 percent recalling actual intercourse.

In Germany, the Institut für Kindheit has recently concluded a survey asking West Berlin schoolchildren about their sexual experiences, and 80 percent reported having been molested.

Outside the West, the sexual molestation of children is a routine practice in most families. Childhood in India begins, according to observers, with the child being regularly masturbated by the mother, the girl "to make her sleep well," the boy "to make him manly." The child sleeps in the family bed, witnesses and most likely takes part in sexual intercourse between the parents. The child is often "borrowed" to sleep with other members of the extended household, leading to the Indian proverb that "For a girl to be a virgin at ten years old, she must have neither brothers nor cousin nor father." Childhood is so eroticized that, as one Western observer put it, "The little Hindu girls are deflowered by the little boys with whom they play, and repeat together the erotic lessons which their parents have unwittingly taught them on account of the general promiscuity of family life throughout India. In all the little girls of less than ten years of age the complete hymen is wanting...Incest is often the rule rather than the exception."

Child marriage was, of course, a long-standing Indian practice. When laws were passed in 1929 trying to outlaw it, the government was overwhelmed by men insisting that early marriage was an absolute necessity, since little girls were naturally very sexual and must be married early if they are to be restrained from seducing adults. "Cupid overtakes the hearts of girls...at an early age," they said. "A girl's desire for sexual intercourse is eight times greater than that of males."

Indian mothers also often supported early marriage, frankly admitting it was necessary in order to protect their little girls against rape in the family, saying that "they were afraid to leave their daughters at home, even for one afternoon, without a mother's eye and accessible to the men of the family."

The Indian subcontinent, in fact, still has many groups, such as the Baiga, where actual incestuous marriage is practiced, between fathers and daughters, between mothers and sons, between siblings and even between grandparents and their grandchildren--thus disproving the oft-repeated anthropological truism that "no known tribe has ever permitted incest" because if it were allowed society would surely cease functioning. In many of these villages, the children move at the age of 5 or 6 from the incestuous activities of the family bed to spend the rest of their childhood in sex dormitories, where they are initiated by older youth and men into intercourse with a succession of other children, none for longer than three days at a time, under threat of gang rape.

Childhood in China has historically had the same institutionalized rape rituals as in India, including the pederasty of boys, child concubinage, the castration of boys to be used sexually as eunuchs, marriage of young girls to a number of brothers, widespread boy and girl prostitution and the regular sexual use of child servants and slaves. So prevalent was the rape of little girls that Western doctors found that, as in India, few girls entering puberty had intact hymens. Even the universal practice of foot binding was for sexual purposes, with a girl undergoing extremely painful crushing of the bones of her feet for years in order that men could make love to her big toe as a fetish, a penis-substitute.

Childhood in contemporary Japan, although somewhat more Western than that of other Eastern nations, still includes masturbation by mothers "to put them to sleep." Parents often have intercourse with their children in bed with them, and "co-sleeping," with parents physically embracing the child, often continues until the child is ten or fifteen. One recent Japanese study found daughters sleeping with their fathers over 20 percent of the time after age 16. Recent sex surveys report memories of sexual abuse even higher than comparable American studies, and "hot lines" of sexual abuse report mother-son incest in almost a third of the calls, the mother saying to her teenage son, "It's not good to do it alone.

Your IQ becomes lower. I will help you, " or "You cannot study if you cannot have sex. You may use my body," or "I don't want you to get into trouble with a girl. Have sex with me instead." Historically, Japan has been one of the most endogamous societies in the world, with incestuous marriages in court circles being approved even in historical times and preferred sibling, cousin, uncle-niece and aunt-nephew marriages having been so extensive that genetics experts have discovered that the incestuous inbreeding has affected the size and health of the Japanese. Even today, there are rural areas in Japan where fathers marry their daughters when the mother has died or is incapacitated, "in accordance with feudal family traditions."

The sexual use of children in the Near East is as widespread as in the Far East. Historically, all the institutionalized forms of pedophilia which were customary in the Far East are documented extensively for the Near East, including child marriage, child concubinage, temple prostitution of both boys and girls, parent-child marriage (among the Zoroastrians), sibling marriage (quite common among Egyptians), sex slavery, ritualized pederasty and child prostitution. Masturbation in infancy is said to be necessary "to increase the size" of the penis, and older siblings are reported to play with the genitals of babies for hours at a time.

Mutual masturbation, fellatio and anal intercourse are also said to be common among children, particularly with the older boys using younger children as sex objects. The nude public baths (hammam) are particularly eroticized in many areas, being especially notorious as a place of homosexual acts, both male and female.

Girls are used incestuously even more often than boys, since females are valued so little. One report found 80 percent of Near Eastern women surveyed recalled having been forced into fellatio between the ages of 3 and 6 by older brothers, cousins, uncles and teachers. The girls rarely complain, since "if there is any punishment to be meted out, it will always end up by being inflicted on her." Arab women know that their spouses are pedophiles and prefer having sex with children to having sex with them. Their retribution comes as follows. When the girl is about 6 years old, the women of the house grab her, pull her thighs apart and cut off her clitoris and often also her labia with a razor, thus usually ending her ability to feel sexual pleasure forever. One Egyptian woman relates her memory of how it happened to her. After being used sexually by the men in her family during her early childhood, she says:

I was six years old that night when I lay in my bed, warm and peaceful...I felt something move under the blankets, something like a huge hand...another hand was clapped over my mouth to prevent me from screaming.

They carried me to the bathroom...I remember...a rasping metallic sound which reminded me of the butcher when he used to sharpen his knife...My blood was frozen in my veins...my thighs had been pulled wide apart...I felt that the rasping knife or blade was heading straight down towards my throat. Then suddenly the sharp metallic edge seemed to drop between my thighs and there cut off a piece of flesh from my body.

I screamed with pain despite the tight hand held over my mouth, for the pain was not just a pain, it was like a searing flame that went through my whole body. After a few moments, I saw a red pool of blood around my hips. I did not know what they had cut off from my body, and did not try to find out. I just wept, and called out to my mother for help. But the worst shock of all was when I looked around and found her standing by my side. Yes, it was her, I could not be mistaken, in flesh and blood, right in the midst of these strangers, talking to them and smiling at them.

A recent survey of Egyptian girls and women showed 97 percent of uneducated families and 66 percent of educated families still practiced clitoridectomy. Nor is the practice decreasing--UN reports estimate that more than 74 million females have been mutilated, with "more female children mutilated today than throughout history."

Clitoridectomy, like all sexual mutilations, is, I believe, an act of incest. If it is incest when a father rapes a daughter, it is also incest when parents assault their children by cutting off, sewing up, burning, flaying or gashing their genitals. In all these cases, the child is being used for the sadistic sexual pleasure of the parent. In fact, circumcision ceremonies are often followed by drinking parties that end in intercourse, so sexually arousing is the circumcision---in some areas, the travelling circumcizer is actually accompanied by some prostitutes, who know how sexually excited villages become after the ceremony. Therefore, the practice of sexually mutilating children's genitals---one of the most widespread rituals in the world--by itself makes incest a near-universal trait.

THE DEAFENING SILENCE OF CHILD ABUSE

Stories of abuse are strange. Sometimes they are blazing headlines — '18 month old raped in Kolkata', 'Teenagers rape toddler in Delhi — but mostly, they silently wrap up inside themselves. This is the story of some of those untold stories, the ones that were desperately locked away in the dusty attics of childhood, untouched and uncleaned.

I recently mentioned that I was writing about child sexual abuse to a well-to-do mother of two boys. "But that stuff doesn't impact my boys, right?" she asked hopefully.

Well, before you think that gender, education or income provides insurance against child abuse, consider these facts: one out of every two children in India is sexually abused, most never report it, 52% of the cases are boys. These are staggering statistics, and essentially mean that if any one of us thinks that there has been no child abuse in our family - we are probably wrong.

In an overwhelming majority of cases, the abuser (almost always male) is part of the household. These are uncles, the cook who has been around since before the kids were born, older cousins, tuition teachers and even the family priests. 'Stranger danger' is one thing but how do we tell our children to watch out for faces who are part of the house?

I went to meet Radhika in Mumbai. She works for a MNC and recently moved from Bangalore. "I just couldn't be in the same city as him anymore" she said.

Starting when she was eleven, her mother's brother seduced her. He showed her pornographic videos for weeks while gently reassuring her that what they were doing was totally normal. "At first, he didn't touch my private parts.

He kept showing me videos of other children doing intimate things with adults. I remember he stroked my head, and told me that this is how kids show love to big people," she says dryly. After weeks of graphic pornography, her uncle started to masturbate in front of her. "He did that for many days before having sex with me. And after he did, he soothed me, again gently stroking my head. He told me that this was our special love. I'll never forget him stroking me, kissing me, his special baby." Psychologists call this kind of seduction 'grooming' where an abuser identifies the victim and then spends weeks, maybe months preparing the child and the family for abuse. As the abuser wins the child's trust, he often starts with permissible touching (like stroking the head) and then slowly sexualizes the relationship.

The abuser uses threats ('I'll kill your dog if you tell anyone', 'your mother will stop loving you') as well as bribes. By grooming children, abusers not only gain the child's trust but also decrease the chance of the child disclosing the abuse and increase the chance of repeated access. Radhika says "minutes after having sex with me, my uncle would have tea with my mother" and so, disclosing his abuse seemed like a "confusing betrayal".

While I was in school in Delhi, our Mathematics tutor endeared himself to us, a group of 15-year-old girls. Far from the usual disinterested tuition teachers, he drove with us to school on exam days and was ready with hugs or help depending on our marks.

He bought us treats and knew all our schoolgirl secrets. We were usually in a group (this made our parents much more relaxed about the time he spent with us) and he effortlessly groomed us all. And then despite the herd, he singled out his victims. He began to call my friend for classes alone. While in the group, he asked her to sit separately in the bedroom while the rest of us sat on the dining table. Soon he made his move writing her sexual letters that detailed all that he would soon "teach her".

I'll never forget the first time that I saw those letters – how could the handwriting of our Maths worksheets be formed into these strange words? His advances became more insistent, and her grades started dropping. To her parents, this only signaled one thing: she needed more Maths tuitions. The onslaught continued for two years before she could tell her parents the truth.

Till this day, I'm grateful that she told her parents. Most kids never do. Explaining why children hold on to this deafening silence, Dr. Bhagat, a Senior Psychiatrist at Apollo Hospital, says, "A person who is abused does not have many forums to discuss it. One cannot start discussing abuse experiences when there is no discourse about other things in the family."

He's right. Generations of Indian children have watched their parents remain silent on sexual issues, sweeping anything uncomfortable under the rug and looking away. We learn this silence which is further complicated by a tradition that demands that every child must respect and obey all elders. And so children obey and remain silent, no matter what the elders do.

Gaurav has buried his story in silence for two decades. We connected through a mutual friend in Mumbai and spoke on the phone.

He started talking about how it all started, on his tenth birthday, "All the cousins had come over and we were playing hide and seek. Hiding in the corner of the backdoor stairs, my oldest cousin told me that he did something special with all 'big boys' and that he was going to show me since I was a 'big boy' now."

Gaurav remembers the pain of what followed with his underwear forced down around his knees. "My cousin kept saying 'look, you're liking it' because my organ grew big. I was confused for a long time – was it my fault?" This guilt and self-blame is a common thread across many survivors. Dr. Bhagat says "Some misinterpret their somatic experience of anxiety as sexual arousal. Many will blame themselves. But the reality, in fact, is that the survivor is repetitively saying 'no' [to abuse] in many ways."

I remained quiet on the phone with for a long time after he narrates his story. I don't have the words to fill the silence. And then he says "my cousin always had keys in his pocket that would clink when he mounted me. Till today, I panic when I hear the sound of keys."

Veena Hari of Arpan, a Mumbai-based NGO confirms that sexual abuse is particularly complicated for boys saying that "boys find it more difficult to report abuse. Because of our patriarchal mindset, most people believe that these things cannot happen to boys. But many incidents occur including inappropriate touching, bullying and same sex exploration." I cringe thinking back to scandals of priests molesting thousands of boys in the Catholic Church. But why go so far as the Vatican – local priests have so much in common with them. A survivor of child abuse describes how her trusted family priest molested her while pretending to 'cleanse' her of black magic. She was at her grandmother's house with her family in the next room.

The good news is that child abuse is largely preventable. But the burden of prevention has rested for too long on our children's tiny shoulders. We have to take charge of prevention by talking about sexual abuse to our children early and often. Pedophiles have themselves said that they would find it much harder to abuse children who were aware of abuse. Talking to children about body parts and inappropriate touching is an important first step that needs to be refreshed every few months. We also need to break our cultural taboo on sex and talk about it appropriately but openly with our children. And while we teach our children to respect their elders, lets also teach them to scream loudly if their elders do something hurtful. And yes, its okay for boys to cry and scream too.

But despite our best efforts, not all children will be protected and not all children will scream loudly. In fact, many survivors say that they quietly "froze" during the abuse. 'Freeze' is one of the brain's survival modes along with 'fight' and 'flight'.

In this mode, many body systems shut down including the hippocampus, the part of the brain that stores memories. As a result, many children don't recall the whole incident but instead remember disjointed details such as the smell of cigarette smoke in the room or the painting on the opposite wall. Or like Gaurav, the clinking of keys.

And so, we can't afford to ignore any statement – no matter how disjointed – from our children. Because when children tell us their story, often vague and fragmented, it is their truth.

Very few reported incidents are false and so, every odd statement made by a child deserves to be investigated by a parent. But while we investigate the problem, we have to reassure our children. A parent's support is the single best predictor of a child's recovery, and our first words of reassurance – without fear, sadness or anger – will set the tone for recovery.

Luckily, we now have a strong law in place – the Protection of Children from Sexual Offences (POSCO) Act – which passed in 2012. But many police and medical personnel still need to be sensitized on it. Authorities often tell parents not to report abuse but even one child's silence is massively dangerous because on average a single molester will abuse 48 more victims.

Despite this risk, police and doctors make statements like "the child's hymen is torn. Don't report it. No one will marry her." The subtext of these statements is that quintessential Indian fear – *log kya kahenge?*

CHILD SEXUAL ABUSE IN INDIA

Child Sexual Abuse is a major problem in India, . This page is a compilation of statistics and major incidents and policy developments around the issue of Child Sexual Abuse in India.

Definition

The Protection of Children from Sexual Offences Act, 2012, drafted to effectively address sexual abuse and sexual exploitation of children, defines different forms of sexual abuse, as listed below:

Penetrative sexual assault

- inserting any object or using any part of body to cause penetration into any part of the body of the child or making the child do so.

Sexual assault without penetration

- touching penis, vagina, anus, breast of a child with sexual intent
- making physical contact to child with sexual intent or making the child do so.

Sexual harassment

- making any sound or gesture or exhibiting any object or part of body, with sexual intent, so that it will be heard or seen by the child
- making a child exhibit his body or make a gesture son that it is seen by the child or other person with sexual intent.
- constantly following or watching child either directly or through digital or any other means with sexual intent

- showing any object to child in any form with sexual intent or enticing child for pornographic purposes.

The law deems a sexual assault to be "aggravated" under certain circumstances, such as when the abused child is mentally ill or when the abuse is committed by a person in a position of trust or authority vis-a-vis the child, like a family member, police officer, teacher, or doctor.

Surveys and statistics

A statement released by Louis-Georges Arsenault, UNICEF Representative to India states, "It is alarming that too many of these cases are children. One in three rape victims is a child. More than 7,200 children including infants are raped every year; experts believe that many more cases go unreported. Given the stigma attached to rapes, especially when it comes to children, this is most likely only the tip of the iceberg."

1998

The Indian NGO Recovery and Healing from Incest (RAHI) conducted India's first study of child sexual abuse. It surveyed 600 English-speaking middle and upper-class women, 76 percent of whom said they had been abused in childhood or adolescence, 40 percent by at least one family member, most commonly an uncle or cousin.

2006

Tulir-CPHCSA's study in 2006,conducted among 2211 school going children in Chennai,indicates a CSA prevalence rate of 42%.Children of all socio-economic groups were found to be equally vulnerable.while 48% of boys reported having been abused,the prevalence rate among girls was 39%.15 % of both the boys and girls were severely abused

2007

The Indian government backed a survey of 125000 children in Thirteen states. Of the children interviewed, more than half (53%) said that they had been subjected to one or more forms of sexual abuse. Over 20% of those interviewed said they were subjected to severe forms of abuse. Of those who said they were sexually abused, 57% were boys.

Law

The government has failed to prevent much of the child sexual abuse from taking place. Additionally, the existing systems of child protection and the stakeholders involved including police, lawyers, media, teachers, parents etc. are simply not doing enough to help victims or to ensure that perpetrators are punished. A government appointed committee, in January, found that the government's child protection schemes, "have clearly failed to achieve their avowed objective."

Causes

It is argued that the prevalence is driven by a higher reluctance to expose relatives and other known persons, who are often the abusers, such as neighbors, teachers and authority figures. As a result, more than 50% of adults who were abused surveyed wanted the matter to stay within the family and only 17% wanted harsh punishments for offenders. There is a culture of silence around it.

Prominent cases

Mathura Rape Case

The Mathura rape case was an incident of custodial rape in India on 26 March 1972, wherein Mathura, a tribal girl who was a minor at the time, was allegedly raped by two policemen on the compound of Desai Ganj Police Station in Chandrapur district of Maharashtra. After the Supreme Court acquitted the accused, there was public outcry and protests, which eventually led to amendments in Indian rape law via The Criminal Law (Second Amendment) Act 1983 (No. 46)

Bharwada Bhoginbhai Hirjibhai v. State of Gujarat 1983

The accused, a middle aged man had confined 2 friends of his daughter aged around 10, who had come to his house to meet the daughter, and had raped them.The trial court convicted the accused for rape, violating modesty and wrongful confinement. The High Court upheld conviction while reducing the charge from rape to attempt to rape. The Supreme Court upheld the judgement of the trial court on the ground that minor discrepancies in the evidence were not relevant. The Court further remarked that corroboration for conviction in rape cases is not necessary. This judgement was relied on in later judgments to secure conviction when they were no other eyewitnesses to support evidence given by the victim.

State of Punjab Vs. Gurmit Singh 1996

In this case, the Supreme Court was highly critical of the acquittal of persons accused of gang-raping a 16-year-old girl. The trial court had referred to the young village girl as a person of loose character who had invented the story of rape to justify spending a night out of home. It had refused to rely on her statement.

The Supreme Court observed that the appreciation of evidence by the trial court was "not only unreasonable but perverse". It held that: *"The testimony of the victim in such cases is vital and unless there are compelling reasons which necessitate looking for corroboration of her statement, the courts should find no difficulty to act on the testimony of a victim of sexual assault alone to convict an accused where her testimony inspires confidence and is found to be reliable. Seeking corroboration of her statement before relying upon the same, as a rule, in such cases amounts to adding insult to injury."*

Sakshi Vs. Union of India 2004

The NGO Sakshi filed a writ petition in Public Interest to broaden the definition of rape in cases involving children where the child is abused by insertion of objects into the vagina or insertion of the male organ into body parts such as anus or mouth. The Supreme Court rejected the Plea & dismissed the PIL. But it issued valuable guidelines for trial of rape and sexual abuse which concern children. These are known as the Sakshi guidelines:-

- A screen or an arrangement where victim or witnesses do not see the body or face of the accused.

- Questions put in cross examination on behalf of accused, if they relate directly to the incident, must be given in writing to the Presiding Officer of the court who may put them to the victim/witnessed in a language that is clear and not embarrassing.
- Victims of child abuse or rape should be allowed sufficient breaks as and when required during the testimony.

Anchorage Case 2006

Duncan Grant, a charity worker and UK citizen, had set up Anchorage shelter in Colaba, Mumbai, in 1995. Allan Waters, another UK citizen, was a visitor to the home. The pair were charged in 2001 with sexual assault after five boys complained to the police about repeated sexual and physical abuse by the men.

They were acquitted by the High Court in Mumbai in 2008 for lack of evidence. But the Supreme Court overturned that decision and upheld guilty verdicts from the trial court in 2006 which sentenced the men to six years.

After POCSO

The Protection of Children from Sexual Offences Act, 2012 received the President's assent on 19 June 2012 and was notified in the Gazette of India on 20 June 2012. The Act is due to come into force shortly, along with the rules being framed under the Act.

State of Maharashtra Vs. Dattatraya

Accused was found guilty under POCSO and awarded the death penalty. Accused was neighbor of the victim, age 5 years. He took the victim to his house forcibly had vaginal & anal sex, caused her head injuries and smothered her as a result of which she died.

Sarath Chandra Pottala V. Union of India

Petitioner challenged the constitutional validity of POCSO on the grounds that if a question arises over the age of the accused, the Special Court has the power to determine the same. However it has no power to seek determination of the age of the victim if there is a dispute regarding it. The petition was dismissed in view of article 15 (3) of constitution and beneficial nature of POCSO.

CHILD SEXUAL ABUSE IN PRODUCTION AND DISTRIBUTION

Children of all ages, including infants, are abused in the production of pornography. The United States Department of Justice estimates that pornographers have recorded the abuse of more than one million children in the United States alone. There is an increasing trend towards younger victims and greater brutality; according to Flint Waters, an investigator with the federal Internet Crimes Against Children Task Force, "These guys are raping infants and toddlers. You can hear the child crying, pleading for help in the video. It is horrendous." According to the World Congress against Commercial Sexual Exploitation of Children, "While impossible to obtain accurate data, a perusal of the child pornography readily available on the international market indicates that a significant number of children are being sexually exploited through this medium."

The United Kingdom children's charity NCH has stated that demand for child pornography on the internet has led to an increase in sex abuse cases, due to an increase in the number of children abused in the production process. In a study analyzing men arrested for child pornography possession in the United States over a one year period from 2000 to 2001, most had pornographic images of prepubescent children (83%) and images graphically depicting sexual penetration (80%). Approximately 1 in 5 (21%) had images depicting violence such as bondage, rape, or torture and most of those involved images of children who were gagged, bound, blindfolded, or otherwise enduring sadistic sex. More than 1 in 3 (39%) had child-pornography videos with motion and sound. 79% also had what might be termed softcore images of nude or semi-nude children, but only 1% possessed such images alone. Law enforcement found about half (48%) had more than 100 graphic still images, and 14% had 1,000 or more graphic images. Forty percent (40%) were "dual offenders," who sexually victimized children and possessed child pornography.

A recent study in Ireland, undertaken by the Garda Síochána, revealed the most serious content in a sample of over 100 cases involving indecent images of children. In 44% of cases, the most serious images depicted nudity or erotic posing, in 7% they depicted sexual activity between children, in 7% they depicted non-penetrative sexual activity between adults and children, in 37% they depicted penetrative sexual activity between adults and children, and in 5% they depicted sadism or bestiality.

Masha Allen, who was adopted at age 5 from the former Soviet Union by an American man who sexually abused her for five years and posted the pictures on the Internet testified before the United States Congress about the anguish she has suffered at the continuing circulation of the pictures of her abuse, to "put a face" on a "sad, abstract, and faceless statistic," and to help pass a law named for her. "Masha's Law," included in the Adam Walsh Child Protection and Safety Act passed in 2006, includes a provision which allows young people 18 and over to sue in civil court those who download pornographic images taken of them when they were children. "Downloading" includes viewing without actual download; many successful prosecutions are completed through using residual images left on the viewer's computer.

THE ROLE OF THE INTERNET IN PROMOTING CHILD PORNOGRAPHY

The Internet has escalated the problem of child pornography by increasing the amount of material available, the efficiency of its distribution, and the ease of its accessibility. Specifically, the Internet:

- permits access to vast quantities of pornographic images from around the world
- makes pornography instantly available at any time or place
- allows pornography to be accessed (apparently) anonymously and privately
- facilitates direct communication and image sharing among users
- delivers pornography relatively inexpensively

- provides images that are of high digital quality, do not deteriorate, and can be conveniently stored
- provides for a variety of formats (pictures, videos, sound), as well as the potential for real-time and interactive experiences
- permits access to digital images that have been modified to create composite or virtual images (morphing).

Components of the Problem

The problem of Internet child pornography can be divided into three components—the production, distribution, and downloading of images. In some cases, the same people are involved in each stage. However, some producers and/or distributors of child pornography are motivated solely by financial gain and are not themselves sexually attracted to children.

Production

This involves the creation of pornographic images. Collectors place a premium on new child pornography material. However, many images circulating on the Internet may be decades old, taken from earlier magazines and films. Images may be produced professionally, and, in these cases, often document the abuse of children in third-world countries. However, more commonly, amateurs make records of their own sexual abuse exploits, particularly now that electronic recording devices such as digital cameras and web cams permit individuals to create high quality, homemade images. With the advent of multimedia messaging (MMR) mobile phones, clandestine photography of children in public areas is becoming an increasing problem.

Distribution

This involves the uploading and dissemination of pornographic images. These images may be stored on servers located almost anywhere in the world. Distribution may involve sophisticated pedophile rings or organized crime groups that operate for profit, but in many cases, is carried out by individual amateurs who seek no financial reward.

Child pornography may be uploaded to the Internet on websites or exchanged via e-mail, instant messages, newsgroups, bulletin boards, chat rooms, and peer-to-peer (P2P) networks. Efforts by law enforcement agencies and Internet Service Providers (ISPs) to stop the dissemination of child pornography on the Internet have led to changes in offenders' methods.

Child pornography websites are often shut down as soon as they are discovered, and openly trading in pornography via e-mail or chat rooms is risky because of the possibility of becoming ensnared in a police sting operation (e.g., undercover police entering chat rooms posing as pedophiles or as minor children). Increasingly those distributing child pornography are employing more sophisticated security measures to elude detection and are being driven to hidden levels of the Internet.

Downloading

This involves accessing child pornography via the Internet. The images do not need to be saved to the computer's hard drive or to a removable disk to constitute downloading.

In some cases a person may receive spam advertising child pornography, a pop-up link may appear in unrelated websites, or he may inadvertently go to a child pornography website (e.g., by mistyping a key word). In most cases, however, users must actively seek out pornographic websites or subscribe to a group dedicated to child pornography. In fact, it has been argued that genuine child pornography is relatively rare in open areas of the Internet, and, increasingly, those seeking to find images need good computer skills and inside knowledge of where to look. Most child pornography is downloaded via newsgroups and chat rooms. Access to websites and online pedophile groups may be closed and require paying a fee or using a password.

Extent of the Problem

It is difficult to be precise about the extent of Internet child pornography, but all of the available evidence points to it being a major and growing problem. At any one time there are estimated to be more than one million pornographic images of children on the Internet, with 200 new images posted daily. One offender arrested in the U.K. possessed 450,000 child pornography images. It has been reported that a single child pornography site received a million hits in a month. As noted above, one problem in estimating the number of sites is that many exist only for a brief period before they are shut down, and much of the trade in child pornography takes place at hidden levels of the Internet. It has been estimated that there are between 50,000 and 100,000 pedophiles involved in organized pornography rings around the world, and that one-third of these operate from the United States.

Profile of Users

There is no one type of Internet child pornography user, and there is no easy way to recognize an offender. Having a preconceived idea of a child sex offender can be unhelpful and prove a distraction for investigating police. Users of Internet child pornography:

- are not necessarily involved in hands-on sexual abuse of children. It is not known exactly how many people may access child pornography on the Internet without ever physically abusing a child. Before the Internet, between one-fifth and one-third of people arrested for possession of child pornography were also involved in actual abuse. However, the Internet makes it easy for people who may never have actively sought out traditional forms of child pornography to satisfy their curiosity online and this may encourage casual users. Looking at the relationship from the other direction, those convicted of sexually abusing children will not necessarily seek out or collect child pornography, with one study putting the number of offenders who do so at around 10 percent. The term child molester covers a wide variety of offenders, from serial predators to situational offenders who may not have ingrained sexual interest in children.
- may come from all walks of life and show few warning signs. In fact, users of child pornography on the Internet are more than likely to be in a relationship, to be employed,

to have an above average IQ, to be college educated, and to not have a criminal record. Those arrested for online child pornography crimes have included judges, dentists, teachers, academics, rock stars, soldiers, and police officers. Among the few distinguishing features of offenders are that they are likely to be white, male, and between the ages of 26 and 40, and may be heavy Internet users to the extent that it interferes with other aspects of their lives.

A PSYCHOLOGICAL TYPOLOGY

Sexual attraction to children is known as pedophilia. However, an interest in Internet child pornography may be best thought of as falling along a continuum rather than in terms of a hard and fast distinction between pedophiles and non-pedophiles. People can behave very differently on the Internet than they do in other areas of their lives. Interacting anonymously with a computer in the safety of one's own home encourages people to express hidden thoughts and desires. Offenders vary in the strength of their interest in child pornography, as well as in the level of severity of the pornographic image to which they are attracted. From a psychological perspective, based on a typology of general pornography users, the following categories of Internet child pornography users are suggested:

1. Recreational users: They access child pornography sites on impulse, out of curiosity, or for short-term entertainment. They are not seen to have long-term problems associated with child pornography use.
2. At-risk users: They are vulnerable individuals who have developed an interest in child pornography, but may not have done so had it not been for the Internet.
3. Sexual compulsives: They have a specific interest in children as sexual objects and seek out child pornography.

An Offending Typology

Variations among offenders translate into different patterns of Internet behavior. Offenders vary in the level of their involvement in Internet child pornography, the degree of networking in which they engage with other offenders, their expertise in employing security strategies to avoid detection, and the extent to which their Internet behavior involves direct sexual abuse of children.

The following typology of child pornography offending has been suggested:

1. Browsers: Offenders who stumble across child pornography but knowingly save the images. They are not involved in networking with other offenders and do not employ security strategies to avoid detection. Their browsing is an indirect abuse of children.
2. Private fantasizers: Offenders who create digital images (e.g., through morphing) for private use to satisfy personal sexual desires. These offenders do not network with other offenders, do not employ security strategies, and their private fantasies are an indirect abuse of victims.
3. Trawlers: Offenders who seek child pornography on the web through open browsers. They may engage in minimal networking, but they employ few security strategies and their trawling is an indirect abuse of victims.
4. Non-secure collectors: Offenders who seek child pornography in non-secure chat rooms (i.e., chat rooms that do not employ security barriers such as passwords) and other open levels of the Internet. They are involved in relatively high levels of networking, and, by definition, do not employ security strategies. Their collecting behavior is an indirect abuse of children. Because of the non-secured nature of their activities, there are limits to the number and nature of the images they can collect.
5. Secure collectors: Offenders who are members of a closed newsgroup or other secret pedophile ring. They engage in high levels of networking and employ sophisticated security measures to protect their activities from detection. Their collecting behavior is an indirect abuse of children. Because they occupy hidden levels of the Internet, they have access to a wide range of images. They may engage in obsessive levels of collecting, which not only involves

amassing huge numbers of images, but also carefully cataloging and cross referencing them. As with other types of collections, they may expend considerable effort in obtaining rare and highly prized images. The collection may become an end in itself.

6. Groomers: Offenders who develop online relationships with children and send pornography to children as part of the grooming process. Grooming involves direct abuse of children. They may or may not be involved in wider networking with other offenders, but their contact with children exposes them to risk of detection. The child may tell someone about the relationship, or the offender may be unwittingly communicating with an undercover police officer.
7. Physical abusers: Offenders who sexually abuse children and for whom an interest in child pornography is just part of their pedophilic interests. They may record their own abuse behaviors for their personal use, in which case, from a legal standpoint, the possession of pornography is secondary to the evidence of their abusive behavior that it records. They may or may not network. By definition, a physical abuser directly abuses victims and his security depends upon the child's silence.
8. Producers: Offenders who record the sexual abuse of children for the purpose of disseminating it to others. The extent of their networking varies depending on whether they are also distributors. Again the producer's direct abuse of the victim compromises his security.
9. Distributors: Offenders involved in disseminating abuse images. In some cases they have a purely financial interest in child pornography. More often, offenders at any of the above levels who share images may be classified as distributors. Thus, the extent of a distributor's networking, his level of security, and whether he engages in direct abuse of children depends upon the level at which he is operating.

CHALLENGES IN CONTROLLING INTERNET CHILD PORNOGRAPHY

Internet child pornography presents some unique challenges for law enforcement agencies. These challenges include:

- The structure of the Internet: The structure of the Internet makes control of child pornography very difficult. The Internet is a decentralized system with no single controlling agency or storage facility. Because it is a network of networks, even if one pathway is blocked, many alternative pathways can be taken to reach the same destination. Similarly, if one website or newsgroup is closed down, there are many others that can instantaneously take its place. The decentralized nature of the Internet, and resultant difficulties in restricting the distribution of child pornography, is exemplified by P2P networks involving direct connections among computers without the need for a central server. It has been argued that the Internet is the ultimate democratic entity and is essentially ungovernable.
- The uncertainties of jurisdiction: The Internet is an international communication tool that crosses jurisdictional boundaries. Not only is cooperation among law enforcement agencies necessary to track offenders across jurisdictions, it is required to coordinate resources and avoid duplication of effort. Parallel operations run from different jurisdictions may unknowingly target the same organization or offender. Equally problematic is the issue of who is responsible for investigating child pornography on the Internet when there is no clue as to where the images originate. There is a potential for pornography crimes to go uninvestigated because they do not fall within a particular law enforcement jurisdiction.
- The lack of regulation: The Internet, by its nature, is difficult to regulate, but many jurisdictions are reluctant to introduce laws that might help control Internet use. There are debates about the appropriate weight to give to the community's protection on the one hand, and to freedom of speech and

commercial interests on the other. There is also legal ambiguity about whether ISPs should be liable for the material they carry (as are television stations) or merely regarded as the conduits for that material (similar to the mail service). The end result is that ISPs' legal obligations with respect to Internet child pornography are often unclear, and, for the most part, the emphasis has been on self-regulation.

- The differences in legislation: To the extent that there have been attempts to regulate the Internet, control efforts are hampered by cross-jurisdictional differences in laws and levels of permissiveness regarding child pornography. For example, in the United States a child is defined as someone under 18; in Australia the age is 16. Moreover, countries vary in their commitment to enforce laws and act against offenders, either for cultural reasons or because of corruption.
- The expertise of offenders: As the typology of Internet offending behavior suggests, offenders vary in the degree to which they employ elaborate security measures to avoid detection. There is a core of veteran offenders, some of whom have been active in pedophile newsgroups for more than 20 years, who possess high levels of technological expertise. Pedophile bulletin boards often contain technical advice from old hands to newcomers. It has been argued that many Internet sting operations succeed only in catching inexperienced, low-level offenders.
- The sophistication and adaptation of Internet technology: The expertise of offenders is enhanced by the rapid advances in Internet technology. In addition to P2P networks, recent developments include remailers (servers that strip the sender's identity from e-mail) and file encryption (a method of hiding or scrambling data). A technological race has developed between Internet pornographers and law enforcement agencies.
- The volume of Internet activity: The sheer amount of traffic in child pornography makes the task of tracking down

every person who visits a child pornography site impossible. Many offenders realize that realistically their chances of being caught are quite remote. Similarly, while perhaps worthwhile activities, catching peripheral offenders or disrupting individual networks may have little overall impact on the scale of the problem.

RESPONSES TO THE PROBLEM OF INTERNET CHILD PORNOGRAPHY

Your analysis of your local problem should give you a better understanding of the factors contributing to it. Once you have analyzed your local problem and established a baseline for measuring effectiveness, you should consider possible responses to address the problem.

The following response strategies provide a foundation of ideas for addressing your particular problem. These strategies are drawn from a variety of research studies and police reports. Several of these strategies may apply to your community's problem. It is critical that you tailor responses to local circumstances, and that you can justify each response based on reliable analysis. In most cases, an effective strategy will involve implementing several different responses. Law enforcement responses alone are seldom effective in reducing or solving the problem. Do not limit yourself to considering what police can do: carefully consider whether others in your community share responsibility for the problem and can help police respond to it.

RELATION TO CHILD MOLESTATION AND ABUSE

Experts differ over any causal link, with some experts saying that use of child porn reduces the risk of offending, and others arguing that it increases the risk. A 2008 American review of the use of Internet communication to lure children outlines the possible links to actual behaviour regarding the effects of Internet child pornography.

According to one paper from the Mayo Clinic of the U.S.A. based on case reports of those under treatment, 30% to 80% of individuals who viewed child pornography and 76% of individuals who were arrested for Internet child pornography had molested a child. As the total number of those who view such images can not be ascertained, the ratio of passive viewing to molestation remains unknown. The report also notes that it is not possible to define the progression from computerized child pornography to physical acts against children.

Several professors of psychology state that memories of child abuse are maintained as long as visual records exist, are accessed, and are "exploited perversely."

Typology

In the late 1990s, the COPINE project ("Combating Paedophile Information Networks in Europe") at University College Cork, in cooperation with thePaedophile Unit of the London Metropolitan Police, developed a typology to categorize child abuse images for use in both research and law enforcement. The ten-level typology was based on analysis of images available on websites and internet newsgroups. Other researchers have adopted similar ten-level scales. In 2002 in the UK, the Sentencing Advisory Panel adapted the COPINE scale to five levels and recommended its adoption for sentencing guidelines, omitting levels 1 to 3 and recommending that levels 4 to 6 combine as sentencing level 1 and that the four levels from 7 to 10 each form an individual severity level, for a total of 5 sentencing stages.

Internet Proliferation

Philip Jenkins notes that there is "overwhelming evidence that [child pornography] is all but impossible to obtain through nonelectronic means." The Internet has radically changed how child pornography is reproduced and disseminated, and, according to the United States Department of Justice, resulted in a massive increase in the "availability, accessibility, and volume of child pornography." The production of child pornography has become very profitable and is no longer limited to paedophiles.

Digital cameras and Internet distribution facilitated by the use of credit cards and the ease of transferring images across national borders has made it easier than ever before for users of child pornography to obtain the photographs and videos. The NCMEC estimated in 2003 that 20% of all pornography traded over the Internet was child pornography, and that since 1997 the number of child pornography images available on the Internet had increased by 1500%.

In 2007, the British-based Internet Watch Foundation reported that child pornography on the Internet is becoming more brutal and graphic, and the number of images depicting violent abuse has risen fourfold since 2003. The CEO stated "The worrying issue is the severity and the gravity of the images is increasing. We're talking about prepubescent children being raped." About 80 percent of the children in the abusive images are female, and 91 percent appear to be children under the age of 12. Prosecution is difficult because multiple international servers are used, sometimes to transmit the images in fragments to evade the law.

Some child pornographers also circumvent detection by using viruses to illegally gain control of computers on which they remotely store child pornography. In one case, a Massachusetts man was charged with possession of child pornography when hackers used his computer to access pornographic sites and store pornographic pictures without his knowledge. The U.S. Court of Appeals for the Tenth Circuit has ruled that if a user downloads child pornography from a file sharing network and possesses it in his "shared folder" without configuring the software to not share that content, he can be charged with distributing child pornography.

Regarding internet proliferation, the U.S. Department of Justice states that "At any one time there are estimated to be more than one million pornographic images of children on the Internet, with 200 new images posted daily." They also note that a single offender arrested in the U.K. possessed 450,000 child pornography images, and that a single child pornography site received a million hits in a month. Further, that much of the trade in child pornography takes place at hidden levels of the Internet, and that it has been estimated that there are between 50,000 and 100,000 paedophiles involved in organised pornography rings around the world, and that one third of these operate from the United States.

In 2008, the Google search engine adapted a software program in order to faster track child pornography accessible through their site. The software is based in a pattern recognition engine.

Collection by Pedophiles

Viewers of child pornography who are pedophiles are particularly obsessive about collecting, organizing, categorizing, and labeling their child pornography collection according to age, gender, sex act and fantasy. According to FBI agent Ken Lanning, "collecting" pornography does not mean that they merely view pornography, but that they save it, and "it comes to define, fuel, and validate their most cherished sexual fantasies." An extensive collection indicates a strong sexual preference for children, and if a collector of child pornography is also a pedophile, the owned collection is the single best indicator of what he or she wants to do. The National Society for the Prevention of Cruelty to Children describes researchers Taylor and Quayle's analysis of pedophile pornography collecting:

"The obsessive nature of the collecting and the narrative or thematic links for collections, led to the building of social communities on the internet dedicated to extending these collections. Through these 'virtual communities' collectors are able to downgrade the content and abusive nature of the collections, see the children involved as objects rather than people, and their own behaviour as normal: It is an expression of 'love' for children rather than abuse."

These offenders are likely to employ elaborate security measures to avoid detection. The US DOJ notes that "there is a core of veteran offenders, some of whom have been active in pedophile newsgroups for more than 20 years, who possess high levels of technological expertise," also noting that pedophile bulletin boards often contain technical advice from child pornography users' old hands to newcomers."

7

Child Protection

Child protection refers to the protection of children from violence, exploitation, abuse and neglect. Article 19 of the UN Convention on the Rights of the Child provides for the protection of children in and out of the home. Child protection systems are a set of usually government-run services designed to protect children and young people who are underage and to encourage family stability.

While there is no universally agreed upon definition, UNICEF defines a 'child protection system' as: the set of laws, policies, regulations and services needed across all social sectors – especially social welfare, education, health, security and justice – to support prevention and response to protection-related risks. These systems are part of social protection, and extend beyond it. At the level of prevention, their aim includes supporting and strengthening families to reduce social exclusion, and to lower the risk of separation, violence and exploitation. Responsibilities are often spread across government agencies, with services delivered by local authorities, non-State providers, and community groups, making coordination between sectors and levels, including routine referral systems, a necessary component of effective child protection systems.

Encountered problems and Child labour

Due to economical reasons, especially in poor countries, children are forced to work in order to survive. Child labour often happens in difficult conditions, which are dangerous and impair the education of the future citizens and increase vulnerability to adults. It is hard to know exactly the age and number of children who work. At least 150 million children under 5 years of age worked in 2004, but the figure is underestimated because domestic labour is not counted.

Endangerment and infanticide

In some countries, children can be imprisoned for common crimes. In some countries, like Iran or China, criminals can even be sentenced to capital punishment for crimes committed while they were children (the United States abandoned the practice in 2005). In contexts where military use of children is made, they also risk being prisoners of war. Other children are forced to prostitution, exploited by adults for illegal traffic in children or endangered by poverty and hunger. Infanticide today continues at a much higher rate in areas of extremely high poverty and overpopulation, such as parts of China and India. Female infants, then and even now, are particularly vulnerable, a factor in sex-selective infanticide.

Child abuse

Most children who come to the attention of the child welfare system do so because of any of the following situations, which are often collectively termed child abuse. Abuse means abuse of power, exercising a power for a purpose not intended. This includes wilful neglect, knowingly not exercising a power for the purpose it was intended. This is why child abuse is defined as taking advantage of a position of trust having been invested with powers

- Physical abuse, is physical assault or battery on the child. Whilst an assault has some adverse consequence that the victim did not agree to (the difference between surgery and stabbing) the victim agrees to the consequences of battery but the agreement is fraudulent in some way (e.g. unnecessary surgery under false pretences). Physical abuse also harassment, a physical presence intended to provoke fear.
- Child sexual abuse, is sexual assault or battery on the child. The vast majority of physical assaults are a reaction

to a situation involving a specific victim. Sexual assault is predominantly perpetrator gratification against any suitable target. Sexual abuse covers the range of direct and indirect assaults (e.g. imagery) and the means of facilitation such as stalking and internet offences.

- Neglect, including failure to take adequate measures to safeguard a child from harm, and gross negligence in providing for a child's basic needs. Needs are the actions to be taken to protect and provide for the child. Safeguarding is the duty of a person given the powers of responsibility for the child to take the necessary measures to protect the child. If a child is physically or sexually abused then there is an (abusive) person responsible for the assault and a (negligent) person responsible for failing to protect from the assault. In some cases they may be the same.
- Psychological abuse, when meeting the child's needs by taking the necessary steps to protect and provide for the child the child's wishes and feelings must be considered when deciding on delivery of the provision that best serves the child's needs. Wilfully failing to provide in accordance with the child's wishes and feelings, whilst it is in his/her best interests is emotional abuse (intentional infliction of emotional distress) or negligently is emotional neglect (negligent infliction of emotional distress).

Parental responsibility

In 1984 the Council of Europe, the body that supervises the European Convention on Human Rights, make Recommendation R(84) 4 on Parental Responsibilities. These defined parental responsibility as a 'function' duties to be met and powers that can be exercised to meet those duties. Child abuse and neglect is failure by a person with parental responsibility to exercise the powers for the intended purpose, the benefit of the child.

Actions typically include services aimed at supporting at-risk families so they can remain intact to safeguard and promote the welfare of the child, investigation of alleged child abuse and, if necessary, assuming parental responsibility by foster care and adoption services.

Child maltreatment

Services are provided by bodies corporate (or legal personalities). Parental responsibility gives parents and businesses that make provision to children and families equivalent legal entities. This includes public bodies and public bodies that regulate private bodies. This has been described as the partnership between state and family

A position held in a body corporate places a person in a position of trust. Child maltreatment is the neglectful or abusive exercise of power in a position of trust by either by a business in delivery of the products that best serve the child's needs for the parents to provide for the child or by the parents in providing for the child with those products.

Other

A 2014 European Commission survey on child protection systems listed the following categories of children needing help:

- Child victims of sexual abuse/exploitation
- Child victims of neglect or abuse
- Child victims of trafficking
- Children with disabilities
- Children in a situation of migration
- Unaccompanied children in a situation of migration
- Children without parental care/in alternative care
- Children in police custody or detention
- Street children
- Children of parents in prison or custody
- Children in judicial proceedings
- Children in or at risk of poverty
- Missing children (e.g. runaways, abducted children, unaccompanied children going missing)

- Children affected by custody disputes, including parental child abduction
- Children left behind (by parents who move to another EU country for work)
- Children belonging to minority ethnic groups, e.g. Roma
- Child victims of female genital mutilation or forced marriage
- Children who are not in compulsory education or training or working children below the legal age for work
- Child victims of bullying or cyberbullying

CHILD PROTECTION ASSESSMENT

A key part of child protection work is assessment. A particular challenge arises where child protection professionals are assessing families where neglect is occurring. Professionals conducting assessments of families where neglect is taking place are said to sometimes make the following errors:

- Failure to ask the right types of question, including
- Whether neglect is occurring?
- Why neglect is occurring?
- What the situation is like for the child?
- Whether improvement in the family are likely to be sustained?
- What needs to be done to ensure the long-term safety of the child?

Protection programme include:

- Improving the understanding of the situation of vulnerable children in need of care and protection.
- Building children's resilience and supporting their participation in their own protection, including child-led organisations and child-to-child support.
- Promoting diversion from inappropriate or punitive responses and encouraging the reintegration of children who have been stigmatised because of their coping strategies in the absence of effective protection mechanisms.

- Demonstrating the benefits of preventative approaches and early intervention over interventions at a later stage.
- Supporting the development of community-based care and protection systems.
- Support to the co-ordination and integration of services and support to vulnerable children.
- Building the care and protection of children into broader social welfare, poverty reduction and other national development strategies.
- Building the capacity of duty bearers to deliver effective care and protection for children.
- Advocating for legal and policy reform in line with the principles and standards of the United Nations Convention on Rights of the Child.

LEGAL PROVISIONS FOR PROTECTION OF CHILDREN

India has signed a number of international documents and declarations that pertain to the rights of the children. The United Nations Convention on the Rights of the Child (UN CRC) was assented to by India in 1992.

In 2005, the Government of India accepted the two Optional Protocols to the UN CRC, addressing the involvement of children in armed conflict and the sale of children, child prostitution and child pornography.

India also signed the International Conventions on Civil and Political Rights, and on Economic, Social and Cultural Rights.

India is also a signatory to the Convention on the Rights of the Child (CRC) adopted by the UN General Assembly in 1989 prescribing standards to be adhered to by all State parties in securing the best interest of the child and outlines the fundamental rights of children, Convention on the Elimination of All Forms of Discrimination against Women (CEDAW) also applicable to girls under 18 years of age and the SAARC Convention on Prevention and Combating Trafficking in Women and Children for Prostitution.

Constitution Of India

The Constitution of India contains a number of provisions for the protection and welfare of the children. It has empowered the legislature to make special laws and policies to safeguard the rights of the children.

Articles 14, 15, 15(3), 19(1) (a), 21, 21(A), 23, 24, 39(e) 39(f) of the Constitution of India contain provisions for the protection, safety, security and well-being of all it's people, including children.

National Policies

The major policies that have been formulated to ensure child rights and improvement in their status are:

- National Policy for Children, 1974
- National Policy on Education, 1986
- National Policy on Child Labour, 1987
- National Nutrition Policy, 1993
- Report of the Committee on Prostitution, Child Prostitutes and Children of Prostitutes and Plan of Action to Combat
- Trafficking and Commercial Sexual Exploitation of Women and Children, 1998
- National Health Policy, 2002
- National Charter for Children, 2004
- National Plan of Action for Children, 2005

Statutes dealing with the protection of Children

Following Acts were enacted for the welfare and protection of the rights of the children:

The Indian Penal Code, 1860

- Foeticide (Sections 315 and 316)
- Infanticide (Section 315)
- Abatement of Suicide: Abatement to commit suicide of minor (Section 305)

- Exposure and Abandonment: Crime against children by parents or others to expose or to leave them with the intention of abandonment (Section 317)
- Kidnapping and Abduction (Section 360 to Section 369)
- Procurement of minor girls by inducement or by force to seduce or have illicit intercourse (Section 366-A)
- Selling of girls for prostitution (Section 372)
- Buying of girls for prostitution (Section 373)
- Rape (Section 376)
- Unnatural Sex (Section 377).

The Pre-natal Diagnostic Techniques (Regulation and Prevention of Misuse) Act, 1994

This is an Act for the regulation of the use of pre-natal diagnostic techniques and for the prevention of misuse of such techniques for the purpose of prenatal sex determination leading to female foeticide and for matters connected therewith or incidental thereto.

The Juvenile Justice (Care and Protection of Children) Act, 2000

The Juvenile Justice (Care and Protection of Children) Act, 2000 provides for proper care, protection and treatment of children in conflict with law and children in need of care and protection by catering to their development needs, and by adopting a child friendly approach in the adjudication and disposition of matters in the best interest of children and for their ultimate rehabilitation through various institutions established under the Act. Sections 23, 24, 26 of the Act deal with the provisions of child abuse.

The Immoral Traffic (Prevention) Act, 1956

The Immoral Traffic (Prevention) Act (ITPA) deals with the offences related to sexual exploitation of children for commercial purposes and to provide enhanced penalties for offences involving children and minor.

Child Labour (Prohibition and Regulation) Act, 1986

The Child Labour (Prohibition and Regulation) Act, 1986Act provides for elimination of child labour and provides for punishments and penalties for employing children below the age of 14 years in various hazardous occupations and processes.

The Prohibition of Child Marriage Act, 2006

The Prohibition of Child Marriage Act, 2006 was enacted to put a stop to the practice of child marriages in India.

For marriages already contracted, it says that every child marriage shall be voidable at the option of the contracting party who was a child at the time of the marriage.

The Commissions for the Protection of Child Rights Act, 2005

The Act provides for the Constitution of a National and State Commissions for protection of Child Rights in every State and Union Territory.

Protection of Children Against Sexual Offences Act, 2012

The Protection of Children from Sexual Offences Act, 2012 was passed by the Parliament in May, 2012. The Act has been drafted to strengthen the legal provisions for the protection of children from sexual abuse and exploitation. Act defines a child as any person below the age of 18 years and provides protection to all children under the age of 18 years from the offences of sexual assault, sexual harassment and pornography. These offences have been clearly defined for the first time in law. The Act provides for stringent punishments, which have been graded as per the gravity of the offence. The punishments range from simple to rigorous imprisonment of varying periods. There is also provision for fine, which is to be decided by the Court.

An offence is treated as "aggravated" when committed by a person in a position of trust or authority of child such as a member of security forces, police officer, public servant, etc.

Punishments for Offences covered in the Act are:

i. Penetrative Sexual Assault (Section 3) – Not less than seven years which may extend to imprisonment for life, and fine (Section 4)

ii. Aggravated Penetrative Sexual Assault (Section 5) -- Not less than ten years which may extend to imprisonment for life, and fine (Section 6)

iii. Sexual Assault (Section 7) – Not less than three years which may extend to five years, and fine (Section 8)

iv. Aggravated Sexual Assault (Section 9) – Not less than five years which may extend to seven years, and fine (Section 10)

v. Sexual Harassment of the Child (Section 11) – Three years and fine (Section 12)

vi. Use of Child for Pornographic Purposes (Section 13) – Five years and fine and in the event of subsequent conviction, seven years and fine (Section 14 (1))

The Act also provides for the establishment of Special Courts for trial of offences under the Act, keeping the best interest of the child as of paramount importance at every stage of the judicial process. The Act incorporates child friendly procedures for reporting, recording of evidence, investigation and trial of offences.

The Act recognizes that the intent to commit an offence, even when unsuccessful for whatever reason, needs to be penalized. The attempt to commit an offence under the Act has been made liable for punishment for upto half the punishment prescribed for the commission of the offence.

The Act also provides for punishment for abetment of the offence, which is the same as for the commission of the offence. This would cover trafficking of children for sexual purposes.

For the more heinous offences of Penetrative Sexual Assault, Aggravated Penetrative Sexual Assault, Sexual Assault and Aggravated Sexual Assault, the burden of proof is shifted on the accused. This provision has been made keeping in view the greater vulnerability and innocence of children. At the same time, to prevent misuse of the law, punishment has been provided for making false complaint or proving false information with malicious intent.

Such punishment has been kept relatively light (six months) to encourage reporting. If false complaint is made against a child, punishment is higher (one year).

The media has been barred from disclosing the identity of the child without the permission of the Special Court. The punishment for breaching this provision by media may be from six months to one year. For speedy trial, the Act provides for the evidence of the child to be recorded within a period of 30 days. Also, the Special Court is to complete the trial within a period of one year, as far as possible.

To provide for relief and rehabilitation of the child, as soon as the complaint is made to the Special Juvenile Police Unit (SJPU) or local police, these will make immediate arrangements to give the child, care and protection such as admitting the child into shelter home or to the nearest hospital within twenty-four hours of the report.

The SJPU or the local police are also required to report the matter to the Child Welfare Committee within 24 hours of recording the complaint, for long term rehabilitation of the child.

The Act casts a duty on the Central and State Governments to spread awareness through media including the television, radio and the print media at regular intervals to make the general public, children as well as their parents and guardians aware of the provisions of this Act. The National Commission for the Protection of Child Rights (NCPCR) and State Commissions for the Protection of Child Rights (SCPCRs) have been made the designated authority to monitor the implementation of the Act.

INTEGRATED CHILD PROTECTION SCHEME

The Integrated Child Protection Scheme is based on the cardinal principles of "protection of child rights" and "best interests of the child". The ICPS aims to promote the best interests of the child and prevent violations of child rights through appropriate punitive measure against perpetrators of abuse and crimes against children and to ensure rehabilitation for all children in need of care and protection.

It aims to create a protective environment by improving regulatory frameworks, strengthening structures and professional capacities at national, state and district levels so as to cover all child protection issues and provide child friendly services at all levels. The Integrated Child Protection Scheme concretises the Government/State responsibility for creating a system to protect children in the country.

Such a system is influenced by the nature of regulatory frameworks, structures, resources, professionals, and the relationships between them. When the child protection system functions in the best interest of the child, adequate state and voluntary institutions, services and structures are put in place, backed strongly by policies, laws and regulations. Professionals providing services for children are competent and bound by professional standards. Children's views are taken into account.

Principles of ICPS

The following key principles underlie the ICPS approach:

(i) Child protection a shared responsibility: The responsibility for child protection is a shared responsibility of government, family, community, professionals, and civil society. It is important that each role is articulated clearly and understood by all engaged in the effort to protect children. Government has an obligation to ensure a range of services at all levels.

(ii) Reducing child vulnerability: There is a need for a focus on systematic preventive measures not just programmes and schemes to address protection failures at various levels. A strong element of prevention will be integrated into programmes, converging the provisions and services of various sectors on the vulnerable families, like livelihood support (NREGS), SHGs, PDS, health, child day care, education, to strengthen families and reduce the likelihood of child neglect, abuse and vulnerability.

(iii) Strengthen family: Children are best cared for in their own families and have a right to family care and parenting by both parents. Therefore a major thrust will be to strengthen the family capabilities to care for and protect the child by capacity building, family counselling and support services and linking to development and community support services.

(iv) Promote non-institutional care: There is a need to shift the focus of interventions from an over reliance on institutionalization of children and move towards more family and community –based alternatives for care. Institutionalization should be used as a measure of last resort after all other options have been explored.

(v) Intersectoral linkages and responsibilities: Child protection needs dedicated sectoral focus as well as strengthening protection awareness and protection response from other sectors outside the traditional protection sector including in emergencies and HIV/AIDS programming.

(vi) Create a network of services at community level: An appropriate network of essential protection services is required at all levels for supporting children and communities.

(vii) Establishing standards for care and protection: All protection services should have prescribed standards, protocols for key actions and should be monitored regularly. Institutionalisation should be for the shortest period of time with strict criteria being established for residential placement and all cases of institutionalization reviewed periodically.

(viii) Building capacities: Protection services require skilled, sensitive staff, equipped with knowledge of child rights and standards of care and protection. Capacities of all those in contact with children require strengthening on a continuing basis, including families and communities.

(ix) Providing child protection professional services at all levels: There is a need for varied special services for the many situations of child neglect, exploitation and abuse, including for shelter, care, psychological recovery, social reintegration, legal services etc. which have to be professional and child-focused.

(x) Strengthening crisis management system at all levels: First response and coordinated inter-sectoral actions for responding to crisis need to be established and institutionalized.

(xi) Reintegration with family and community: systems to be put in place for efforts to reintegrate children with their families and community and regular review of efforts instituted.

(xii) Addressing protection of children in urban poverty: Children in urban poverty are at high risk/ increased vulnerability; constantly under threat of eviction; denial or exclusion from basic services; social turmoil; and the stretched capacity of the adults to function as adequate caretakers due to their poverty. This indicates the need for developing a strong social support and service system.

(xiii) Child impact monitoring: all policies, initiatives and services will be monitored for their child impact and reports made public, including for children themselves through child-friendly reports.

In order to reach out to all children, in particular to those in difficult circumstances, the Ministry of Women and Child Development proposes to combine its existing child protection schemes under one centrally sponsored scheme titled "Integrated Child Protection Scheme (ICPS)". The proposed ICPS brings together multiple vertical schemes under one comprehensive child protection programme and integrates interventions for protecting children and preventing harm. It does not see child protection as the exclusive responsibility of the MWCD but stresses that other sectors have vital roles to play. The Ministry looks at child protection holistically and seeks to rationalize programmes for creating a strong protective environment for children, diversify and institutionalize essential services for children, mobilize inter-sectoral response for strengthening child protection and set standards for care and services. ICPS will function as a Government

– Civil Society Partnership scheme under the overarching direction and responsibility of the Central/State Governments. It will work closely with all stakeholders including government departments, the voluntary sector, community groups, academia and, most importantly, families and children to create a protective environment for children in the country. Its holistic approach to child protection services and mechanisms is reflected in stronger lateral linkages and complementary systems for vigilance, detection and response. The scheme visualizes a structure for providing services as well as monitoring and supervising the effective functioning of child protection system, involving:

- Government: To hold primary responsibility for the development, funding and operation of the service covered under the scheme. In order to ensure effective functioning of the system, the Government shall provide flexibility by cutting down rigid structures and norms. To attract the best professional talent and strengthen public-private partnership, the scheme proposes to hire services of professionals on a contractual basis.
- Civil society organizations:
  - Voluntary sector: To provide vibrant, responsive and child friendly services for detection, counselling, rehabilitation for all children in need as well as provide technical support; these may be financially supported by the State.
  - Research and training institutions: To carryout activities related to research and capacity building of existing manpower as well as support creation of a cadre of professional manpower.
  - Media and advocacy groups: To promote rights of the child and child protection issues with sensitivity and promote child's dignity and worth ° Corporate sector:
- Community groups and local leaders, youth groups, families and children: To provide protective and corrective environment for children, to act as watchdog and monitor child protection services as well as service providers, both Government and NGO functionaries.

Aim Groups

Child in need of care & protection means a child who:

- is found without any home or settled place or abode and without any ostensible means of subsistence;
- resides with a person (whether a guardian of the child or not) and such person has threatened to kill or injure the child and there is a reasonable likelihood of the threat being carried out, or has killed, abused or neglected some other child or children and there is a reasonable likelihood of the child in question being killed, abused or neglected by that person;
- is a mentally or physically challenged or ill child or a child suffering from terminal diseases or incurable diseases, and/or having no one to support or look after him/her;
- has a parent or guardian and such parent or guardian is unfit or incapacitated to care for or exercise control over the child;
- does not have a parent/parents and no one is willing to take care of him/her, or whose parents have abandoned him/her or who is a missing and/or runaway child and whose parents cannot be found after reasonable inquiry
- is being or is likely to be grossly abused, tortured or exploited for the purpose of sexual abuse or illegal acts
- is found vulnerable and is likely to be inducted into drug abuse or trafficking,
- is being or is likely to be abused for unconscionable gains
- is victim of any armed conflict, civil commotion or natural calamity.

Children in conflict with the law is one who is alleged to have committed an offence. Children in contact with law is one who has come in contact with the law either as victim or as a witness or due to any other circumstance. Any other vulnerable child including, but not limited, to: Children of potentially vulnerable families and families at risk, Children of socially excluded groups like migrant families, families living in extreme poverty, lower caste families, families subjected to or affected by discrimination, minorities, children infected and/or affected by HIV/AIDS, orphans, child drug abusers, children of substance abusers, child beggars, trafficked or sexually exploited children, children of prisoners, and street and working children, would also be covered under the scheme.

Objectives of the scheme:

(i) To create a safety net for children in need of care and protection and children in conflict with law by building a protective environment for them, keeping their best interests in mind;

(ii) To promote preventive measures to protect children from falling in the situations of vulnerability, risk and abuse

(iii) To promote preventive measure to address the vulnerabilities of families and build their ability and capacity protect their children;

(iv) To supplement and strengthen the infrastructure established under the Juvenile Justice (Care and Protection) Act 2000;

(v) To build capacities of families, communities, and NGOs to strengthen care, protection and response to children;

(vi) To create State and District Child Protection Units as well as State Adoption Cells;

(vii) To promote in-country adoption and regulate inter-country adoption as well as ensure minimum standards;

(viii) To provide services to the more vulnerable categories of children through specialized programmes;

(ix) To establish linkages for restoration of children to their biological families and placement with adoptive families or foster families, where necessary;

(x) To provide specialized institutional care to infants and children up to 6 years of age who are either abandoned or orphaned/destitute;

(xi) To check and end female foeticide and infanticide in the country;

(xii) To provide services to street and destitute children, including child beggars;

(xiii) To provide for care and support services for children affected by HIV/AIDS;

(xiv) To establish CHILDLINE in every district, for creating access in emergencies by providing counselling, restoration and rehabilitative services to children along with linkages to other available services under various schemes of the Government of India/State Governments;

(xv) To train and sensitize local bodies, police, judiciary and other concerned departments of State Governments to undertake related responsibilities;

(xvi) To strengthen the knowledge base by undertaking research and documentation, resource mapping of services, the creation of a Management Information System (MIS) for tracking vulnerable children, and database management;

(xvii) To carry out advocacy and spread awareness about child and family-related issues for supporting the family;

(xviii) To network with the Allied Systems i.e. Government departments and Non-Government agencies;

(xix) To initiate any other need-based specialized innovative services through families, community and panchayats/local bodies, including child guidance and counselling, especially to combat drug abuse, sexual abuse, child marriage, and discrimination against the girl child.

Schemes

The ICPS will be guided by the critical child protection strategies and priorities visualized under the National Plan of Action for Children, 2005. These strategies will be based on four major parameters, including:

Prevention Destitution

- Preventing destitution & exploitation of children through care, protection & developmental programmes
- Achieving 100% registration of births, deaths and marriages by 2010

- Establishing support services for families at risk
- Eradication of harmful, traditional and customary practices that put children at risk, particularly of trafficking and sexual exploitation
- Ensuring survival, development and protection of the girls child and restoring her dignity by eliminating harmful, discriminatory and unethical traditional practices, and providing legal, medical, social and psychological support services and opportunities fro development of their full potential
- Ensuring enforcement of all laws relating to children, particularly the Child Marriage Restraint Act, PNDT Act, ITPA, Juvenile Justice (care and Protection of Children) Act, Child Labour (Prohibition and Regulation) Act, amongst others
- Prevention of cross-border trafficking and creation of nodal authorities and other infrastructure to deal with all kinds of child trafficking
- Adoption of a national law to deal with child trafficking, including ratification of the international instruments such as the UN Protocol on Trafficking in Persons
- Ensuring access to mainstream education for all child labourers by 2012 and access to nutrition, clothing and protection from all forms of abuse and neglect
- Elimination of child marriages
- Eliminate disability due to poliomyletis by 2007
- Creation of effective links and quick referrals between ICDS, Primary Health Centres, mother and child programmes and hospitals (paediatric units) for early detection of high risk babies and children with disabilities
- Access to neighbourhood schools and inclusive education, accessible and disable friendly infrastructure, early childhood care for the disabled child, inclusion of children with mental illness in all existing schemes fro children with disability, vocational training, capacity building of

care givers, access to services, support and protection, implementation of the disability law

- Prevention of mother-to-child transmission of HIV/AIDS
- Requisite counselling, awareness generation and support services for adolescents to prevent them for becoming vulnerable and protect them from harm
- Contingency planning and emergency preparedness
- Convergence with related Ministries / Department at Central & State levels
- Enlisting support from the private sector
- Ensuring child specific interventions in all urban planning.

Special Protection

- Special measures for protection of children in urban and semi urban situations
- Special attention to certain categories of children requiring greater focus such as, child beggars, child labour, street children, children in need of care and protection and children in conflict with law as covered by the juvenile justice act, trafficked children, child victims of sexual abuse and exploitation, children affected by natural and man made disasters, children of sex workers and prisoners, children affected by armed conflict and civil disorders.
- Ensuring a supportive and enabling environment for care and protection of children affected by HIV/AIDS
- Quality health care and services, including free Anti-Retroviral therapy for children infected with HIV virus
- Development of special packages for children abandoned on account of HIV/AIDS
- Promoting community based care and rehabilitation for all children in difficult circumstances
- Childline & other necessary support service, infrastructure, referral for children in emergency situations
- Promotion of quality institutional and alternative care

- Up-gradation of standards of existing services
- Infrastructural support to NGOs for destitute, orphan children through incountry adoption
- Combating trafficking of narcotic drugs, psychotropic substance to prevent the use by children and creating Mechanisms for rehabilitation of child substance abusers
- Drop-in-shelters which encourage children's voluntary attendance and participation in activities such as music, theater, yoga & meditation, computers, games and other creative activities so as to ensure their overall development, care and protection and to reduce social deviance
- Implementation of juvenile justice law
- Creation of child-friendly judicial and administrative procedures for dealing with children
- Free legal aid and advice for children in conflict with law
- Assistance to child victims of abuse and exploitation for their full physical and psychological recovery, development and social reintegration
- Institution of a rights based uniform definition of child labour and bonded labour
- Elimination of all forms of child labour by linking it with ensuring right to education for all children
- Convergence with related Ministries / Department at Central & State levels
- Enlisting support from the private sector.

THE BEST INTERESTS OF THE CHILD

Decision making

Decisions made on all the necessary products: environments, accommodation, goods and services procured to be provided for the child's safe consumption must be in the best interests of the child. A child is a person, not an object of concern who simply lacks the capacity to give consent on her own behalf until Gillick Competent to do so. He/she must still be involved in the decision making processes for the products that best serve his/her needs in accordance with the best interests determination of s.4 Mental Capacity Act 2005. Failure of the responsible person to so is an offence on the grounds of emotional neglect.

The welfare checklist

Working Together to Safeguard Children extends mental capacity to parental capacity for a person with parental responsibility and the best interests consideration under s.1(3)(a)-(f) the, so-called, [welfare checklist of family law.

s.1(3)(a) the wishes and feelings of the child in light of his age and experience; are the child's involvement in the decision making process.

s.1(3)(b) the child's physical, emotional and educational needs; are for physical and emotional neglect to be prevented and to receive a proper education (s.36 Children Act 1989) in accordance with his/her aptitudes, abilities and any special needs he may have (s.7 Education Act 1996).

s.1(3)(c) the likely effect of the change of circumstances are the likely outcomes for the child of the products as environment, accommodation, goods and services procured to be provided for him/her.

s.1(3)(d) the age, sex, background, and other relevant characteristics of the child specifies the child's current condition for which the provision is required to address.

s.1(3)(e) harm the child has suffered, or is at risk of suffering; specifies the harm, as ill-treatment or impairment of health and development the child has suffered or the hazards in his/her circumstances from which she is at risk of suffering harm. Just as in employment health and safety, these are the risks of the present care environment.

s.1(3)(f) capability of the parents, or anybody else considered relevant, of meeting the child's needs; is the ability and responsibility of the parents for procuring the necessary products as environments, accommodation, goods and services to promote the child's welfare to be safely provided to him/her in safeguarding his/her welfare.

Decision making and legal disability

There is both a business and social imperative to give all the opportunity for safely and satisfactorily consuming the offerings of producers. Some, may not have the capacity to be capable of giving proper consent or agreement for the products that best serve their needs to use those products safely. In the case of parents, their children's needs to keep their children safe. This is called Legal Disability.

Disability is the difference between capacity and capability. In the case of parents parental capacity of Working Together and parental capability of s.1(3)(f) of the Children Act 1989. Disability is defined as a mental or physical impairment with and adverse effect on normal day-to-day activities. A person without the use of their legs lacks the physical capacity to walk. They are not capable of carrying out the normal day-to-day activity of, say, shopping without some corrective measure such as a mobility scooter.

Mental capacity is the ability to make decisions in a best interests determination on a particular issue so as to be mentally capable of giving proper consent or agreement. Determining mental capacity requires the information on which the decision to be made to safeguard the person's welfare. A lack of mental capacity to process the information and make decisions is a legal disability leaving the person incapable of instructing a solicitor (s.3 Mental Capacity Act 2006, 26 Explanatory Notes to the Mental Capacity Act (2005); 1.6 Family Law Protocol (Law Society 2010)).

Physical, moral and emotional health, the mental faculties of decision making

Physical and moral health refer to the faculties of the mind used in making decisions. Physical health is the mental capacity to understand the effects of matter and energy on both self and others. That is, to understand how a person may be physically harmed which is called causality in the law of negligence. Moral health is the mental capacity to recognise the persons and environment that may be damaged by the acts and omissions in the law of negligence, the neighbour and neighbourhood.

Part 1 of the Children and Young Peoples Act 1933 is headed *"Prevention of Cruelty to Children and Exposure to Physical and Moral Danger"*. The offence of child cruelty under s.1(1) includes *"...exposure in a manner likely to cause an unnecessary injury to health..."*. Again, the manner of the exposure endangers the child's physical and moral health as faculties of the mind. It means nothing more than setting a bad example in either behaviour towards others (moral health) or carelessness with potentially dangerous items, e.g. speeding in a motor car.

Emotional health is firstly intellectual health, the capacity to reason based on the understandings of physical and moral health when making decisions so as not harm a neighbour or neighbourhood. It is secondly the competencies to engage in social relationships, personal or business, under the terms of proper consent or agreement following that reasoning and decision making. Thirdly, it is the likely capability of applying those competencies to take opportunities in the cause of growth and well-being and then to perform reliably.

Child development and parental responsibility

The Department of Health Introduction to the Children Act 1989 described new notion of parental responsibility as *"the authorities conferred by parental responsibility exist only for raising the child to physical, emotional and moral health"*. Lord McKay of the Clasfern, the Lord Chancellor when introducing the act to Parliament said *"...the overwhelming task of parenthood and the all the rights it brings are for raising the child to be a properly developed adult, both physically and morally."*.

The child's physical and moral health are developed as physical development and behavioural (moral) development of physical and moral capacities; the child's emotional health is developed as intellectual development for the capacity to reason based on those understandings when making decisions; social development as the competencies to enter into social relationships, both personal and business; and emotional development of likely capability to take opportunities in the cause of growth and well-being and perform reliably.

"A child is a person not an object of concern"

Lady Elizabeth Butler Sloss made this oft quoted remark in her inquiry into the Cleveland child abuse scandal. As a medical discipline, child welfare under s.1 and s.44 of the Children and Young Peoples Act 1933 is only distinguished from animal welfare under s.9 Animal Welfare Act 2006 by consideration of the child's wishes and feelings when making decisions in her best interests following s.4 Mental Capacity Act 2005 extended to parental capacity by Working Together to Safeguard Children and s.1(3)(a)-(f) of the Children Act 1989.

An animal is a possession whilst a child is a person and this distinction was a central intention of the Children Act 1989. Lord McKay also said when introducing the act, *"The days when a child was regraded as a possession of his family, indeed to sue on their loss, are today buried forever"*. The child is socially and emotionally developed, whilst he lacks capacity, by full involvement in the decision making process in his best interests until he becomes competent as Gillick Competent.

Disability, parental disability and social inclusion

The Department of Work and Pensions disability assessment is a measure of physical and mental capacities under clinical or controlled conditions from occupational health in respect to employment performance. The test for disability is capability as *"the mental or physical impairment with an adverse effect on day-to-day activities"* as social performance. The assessment of capacity is used in a home based disability assessment under s.47 NHS and Community Care Act 1990.

For a parent, a parental disability is the mental or physical impairment with the adverse effect on the day-to-day activity of giving the child the care it would be reasonable to expect a parent to give a similar child (s.31 Children Act 1989).

Whatever their mental or physical impairments parents should be given the necessary disability support to care for their children to maintain a reasonable standard of health and development. (s.17(10) Children Act 1989).

For those with parental responsibility mental capacity to make decisions in own best interests is extended to parental capacity to make decisions in the best interests of the child by Working Together to Safeguard Children. The s.47 disability assessment is extended by Part III and s.8 Part 1 Schedule 2 Children Act 1989.

Part III Children Act 1989 includes s.17 and the local authority duty to safeguard and promote the welfare of children by the provision of services for the families of children in need. The services include advocacy services for advice and assistance in decision making when exercising the authorities of parental responsibility. This was another clear intention of the act described in the Department of Health Introduction as *"...the belief that children are best brought up in the family with both parents playing a full part...the local authority duty to provide support for children and families..."*

The MARAC Process and risk assessment

The s.47 disability assessment is to support mental health care in the community and is conducted with a view to a possible deprivation of liberty for those who lack the capability to care for themselves in the community under Schedule A1 Mental Capacity Act 2005. The decision is made after a Multi Agency Risk Assessment Conference know as MARAC.

In the case a parent who is not capable of meeting the child's needs then the local authority can intervene with a court order under s.31(2) Children Act 1989. To do so they must meet the public law thresholds that the child is suffering, or likely to suffer, significant harm attributable to the care it would be reasonable to expect a parent to give, the same criteria as for parental disability support.

State intervention

It is assumed that the parent has been given the necessary support for any parental disability under the terms of proper consent, that the welfare of the child has been safeguarded and the risk to the child is parental negligence. The test of parental negligence is, following Donoghue later called the Bolam Test, the same test as for professional negligence. If a care order is made the local authority acquires parental responsibility under s.33 of the act as the, so-called, corporate parent.

These thresholds are highly controversial and poorly understood. A number of esoteric legal principles are involved and most easily understood in terms of employment performance and health and safety.

A parent, just like the CEO of a corporate body, must be, and be seen to be a fit and responsible person. If called into question the court will firstly examine the facts. In employment health and safety there are the facts of accidents, the accident record book of harm suffered, and the facts of the employment environment, harm likely to be suffered, say, from a trip hazard.

The facts are found to the civil standard of proof, the balance of probabilities, 'Did the facts of the alleged trip hazard occur?", this is called 'The Trier of Fact'.

If so, do these found facts amount to a trip hazard?, this is called the Question of Law. This conforms that the alleged events occurred and were unlawful but that is not enough there is next the issue of culpability or State of Mind.

Negligence is a state of mind. This notion comes from the criminal law and the offence of child cruelty under s.1 Children and Young Peoples Act 1933. What was the motivation, carelessness or malice? There is a defence of diminished responsibility, the offence occurred but was not voluntary or reasonably foreseeable by an impaired or incapacitated defendant.

The offence of child cruelty allows a defence of parental incapacity on a wide range of grounds.

The employment health and safety approach is again helpful in understanding this complexity. To summarise so far, as a matter of fact found on the balance of probabilities, the child has suffered harm or been exposed to an unsafe environment. The person responsible for the child was in, at least, a negligent state of mind in failing to protect the child to safeguarding or promote his/her welfare.

This is all based in the present and the final finding is as a fit and proper person to hold this responsibility into the future. Is there a track record of such irresponsible behaviour?

Preventing child neglect and abuse

The offence of child cruelty can be prosecuted concurrently with any assault on the child. If a child is assaulted, sexually or physically, then both the assailant and the person responsible for keeping the child safe from the assault are culpable for the harm suffered as physical abuse abuse or sexual abuse. This completes the definitions of child neglect and abuse.

The offence of child cruelty is the UK implementation of Article 19(1) UN Convention on the Rights of the Child *Protection of Children From Violence*. Article 19(2) requires social programmes to for preventing violence to children and these are to be found under s.4 Part 1 Schedule 2 Children Act 1989 and include services to children and families under Part III of the same enactment in meeting the local authority duty to safeguard and promote the welfare of children.

CHILD PROTECTION BY COUNTRY

Most countries have introduced laws to protect and prevent children and young persons from certain threats or harms.

United Kingdom

History

In 1908 the Children Act 1908 was introduced followed by the Children and Young Person Act 1920 with a bundle of laws to protect young persons and children in the early 20th century. The Children and Young Persons Act 1933 consolidated the laws into a single law.

The Children Act 1933 defined child neglect and abuse as is now currently understood in the context of welfare and well-being. Welfare (health, safety and happiness) is the 'fare', nourishment, that makes a person 'well', healthy.

Lucy Delap notes that 'the period before 1948 saw the majority of work with vulnerable children undertaken by 'moral' or family welfare workers. These were mostly voluntary workers based within groups such as the Church of England's Moral Welfare Associations. Their remit also included supporting 'friendless girls', unmarried mothers and babies, intervening to prevent prostitution, and helping treat and prevent the spread of venereal disease. Boys were not widely perceived as sexually vulnerable, and barely featured in discussions of child assault and prostitution.'

Well-being is the personal motivation and aspiration for security, comfort and emotional contentment that drives the process. The offence of child cruelty under section 1 of the Children and Young Peoples Act 1989 provides protection for health and safety. Learning, as the other essential ingredient to the pursuit of well-being, is covered by section 44.

Child protection and the prevention of neglect and abuse follows this model throughout. This was the approach that led the policy imperative for eradicating child poverty in a system of public health epidemiology. A programme international promoted by the World Health Organisation in the Health For All programming goal and nationally as Health for All Children. The public health imperative of well-being is exactly mirrored in the socio-economic philosophy of capabilities as welfare economics.

Whilst the Children and Young People Act 1933 established the foundations they were later consolidated into the state's employment, education, health and welfare by the Children Act 1989 and following tranche of legislation. Internationally, the principles were embodied in the UN Convention on the Rights of the Child.

Important Changes in 1933:

- Minimum age of execution was raised from 16 to 18 years.
- The age of criminal responsibility was raised from 7 to 8 years.
- Introduction of a minimum working age of 14 years.
- The minimum age to smoke and to buy tobacco products was set at 16 years.
- The minimum age for prostitution and to enter a brothel is set at 16 years.

- The minimum age to give alcohol to a child on a private premises is set at 5 years.

Child welfare

The laws of negligence and contract

As can be seen from the above provisions, which all follow the principles of the Children and Young Peoples Act 1933, child protection is concerned with the child's exposure to, and consumption of, potentially hazardous products of all description.

The act followed Donoghue v Stevenson [1932] UKHL 100 to reflect the new law of negligence and demolition of the privily barrier in the law of contract. The new law recognised that the product manufacturer may be *many parties removed* from the ultimate product consumer and that the product may contain potentially hazardous but un-examinable content. This may be either through ingredient or packaging. Food intolerances are a simple example. The purchaser will be unaware of potentiality allergic content unless clearly advised by the producer.

The purchaser, or more generally 'procurer' (person who obtains), of product may not be the ultimate consumer. A parent procures for a child who is, potentially, the most vulnerable consumer. Section 1(1) of the Children and Young Peoples Act 1933 makes it a criminal offence of child cruelty for the person responsible for a child to expose him/her "in a *manner likely to cause him unnecessary suffering or injury to health*" (emphasis supplied).

The approach is no different to employment health and safety, but for the consumer rather than the employee.

It is the *"manner"* of acting that is important: is this activity being carried out safely after an appropriate risk assessment to meet the duty of care in the law of negligence established by Donoghue. The person responsible for a child should know the child's food allergies and check any product content for potential food intolerances before allowing the child to consume the product.

Safeguarding the welfare of the child

Child safeguarding follows directly from these principles.

Safeguarding means taking the necessary protective measures for the child's safe consumption of any product, stair-gates, seatbelts, protective footwear, glasses, basic hygiene, etc. The list is both endless and, to the most part, obvious common sense. Failure by the responsible person is an offence of child cruelty on the grounds of failing to protect the child in circumstances consistent with the provision of safe and effective care .

A parent, person with parental responsibility for a child, has an express liability, whoever is responsible for the child at the time (s.17 of the act). Just as in employment health and safety, the powers of parenthood can be delegated but not the duties. Parents should make arrangements for suitable and properly informed others to have responsibility for their children.

Proper consent or agreement

For the product to be safely consumed by a child means that the responsible person must fully understand the product's safe use for its intended purpose. Miss-selling in the law of contract, suggesting the product does something it doesn't or selling products to those that do not fully understand what they are getting is potentially hazardous to the child as the ultimate consumer. Health and medical treatment may involve some form of physical contact in which case lack of proper consent is a potential battery, or even assault, of the person. The procurer must be placed in a position to assess any potential risk to the child in the reliable use of the product.

Welfare, risk assessment and the calculus of negligence

Just as in all off life, the likely benefits of a procured product. Procurement is a careful activity attempting to achieve the best value for money. The benefits of the product must be satisfactorily delivered as specified for performance in the law of contract. Just as in food intolerances and consent to examination and treatment, the procurer must be made aware of any potential hazards in their circumstances of a product that performs reliably.

Welfare as is health, safety and happiness as satisfaction with performance in the law of contract. Welfare defines the process by which proper consent or agreement is given when procuring products that will be beneficial and safe in the procurer's particular circumstances. If a child is the ultimate consumer of a procured product then the child's welfare (health, safety and happiness) is the paramount consideration when coming to the decision.

A balance must be struck between the obligations of the producer and the obligations of the procurer for the child's safe consumption of the product. The calculus of negligence is a legal approach, in the spirit of procurement efficiency, that attempts to strike that balance on economic grounds. This is most easily understood in terms of insurance liability. Should a car driver have a duty of care towards until cyclists at night or should the cyclist have a duty of care to properly illuminate his bicycle at night? The costs of bicycle illumination are considerably less than the cost of driving with a duty of care to unlit cyclists.

Promoting the welfare of the child and the CAF Assessment

A parent must also procure (obtain) all necessary products, environments, accommodation, goods and services to be provided for the child's safe consumption. Failure to do so is, again, an offence of child cruelty under s.1(2) of the act on the grounds of physical neglect and failing to prevent harm as impairment of health and development in Working Together to Safeguard Children.

The procurement process for integrated provision is called a Children and Family Assessment, CAF Assessment, for integrated provision. The outcome is a CAF Action Plan to safeguard and promote the child's welfare with the specified outcomes of the services that best serve the child's needs to be delivered under the terms of proper consent. In the Family Justice System the CAF Assessment is conducted by the Children and Family Court Advisory and Supervisory Service (CAFCASS) to *safeguard and promote the welfare of children involved in family court proceedings*. In the Youth Justice System and Special Education Needs the CAF Assessment is conducted by local council parental responsibility units following Schedule 2 of the Special Educational Needs Regulations (Consolidated) 2001.

SURVIVING CHILD PROTECTION MECHANISMS

The existing mechanisms for child protection in India primarily flow from the provisions under the Juvenile Justice (Care and Protection of Children) Act, 2000 and National Plan of Action for Children 2005.

These comprise several programmes and schemes implemented by different ministries and departments addressing child protection issues among which are:

- An Integrated Programme for Street Children without homes and family ties. Under the scheme NGOs are supported to run 24 hours drop-in shelters and provide food, clothing, shelter, non-formal education, recreation, counselling, guidance and referral services to them. The other components of the scheme include enrollment in schools, vocational training, occupational placement, mobilizing preventive health services and reducing the incidence of drug and substance abuse, HIV/AIDS etc.
- A Programme for Juvenile Justice for children in need of care and protection and children in conflict with law. The Government of India provides financial assistance to the State Governments/UT Administrations for establishment and maintenance of various homes, salary of staff, food, clothing, etc. for children in need of care and protection and juveniles in conflict with law. Financial assistance is based on proposals submitted by States on a 50-50 cost sharing basis.
- Childline Service for children in distress, especially children in need of care and protection so as to provide them medical services, shelter, rescue from abuse, counselling and repatriation.
- Scheme for Working Children in Need of Care and Protection for children working as domestic help, at roadside dhabas, mechanic shops, etc. The scheme provides for bridge education and vocational training, medicine, food, recreation/sports equipments, etc.

- Shishu Greh Scheme for care and protection of orphans/abandoned/destitute infants or children up to 6 years and promote in-country adoption for rehabilitating them.
- Rajiv Gandhi National Creche Scheme for the Children of Working Mothers in the age group of 0-6 years. The scheme provides for comprehensive day-care services including facilities like food, shelter, medical, recreation, etc.
- Pilot Project to Combat the Trafficking of women and Children for Commercial Sexual Exploitation in source and destination areas for providing care and protection to trafficked and sexually abused women and children. Components of the scheme include networking with law enforcement agencies, rescue operation, temporary shelter for the victims, repatriation to hometown and legal services, etc.

Central Adoption Resource Agency (CARA)

- National Child Labour Project (NCLP) for the rehabilitation of child labour. Under the scheme, Project Societies at the district level are fully funded for opening up of special school/Rehabilitation Centres for the rehabilitation of child labour. These special schools/rehabilitation centres provide non-formal education, vocational training, supplementary nutrition, stipend etc. to children withdrawn from employment.

In early 2006 the Department of Women and Child Development became a full-fledged Ministry and the juvenile justice and adoption related matters were transferred to this new Ministry. However, Child Protection has never been a programme of any one Ministry/Department and in spite of this rationalization, child labour issues continue to be dealt with by the Labour Ministry. However, for Child Protection to be dealt with more effectively there is a need for lateral linkages by the Ministry of Women and Child Development with relevant sectors such as Railways, Industry, Trade and Commerce, Rural Development, Urban Affairs, Tourism, Banking, Legal Affairs, Home Affairs, Health and Family Welfare, and Information and Broadcasting.

Some of the schemes of the Ministry of Women and Child Development under the women's welfare section address issues concerning protection of the girl child even though there is no girl child specific component and budget under these schemes.

These need to be considered as child protection schemes and in the years to come they could perhaps have a clearly defined child protection component and budget.

These schemes include:

- Swadhar
- Scheme for rescue of victims of trafficking
- Short Stay Home
- Relief and rehabilitation of rape victims.

The Kishori Shakti Yojana of Women and Child

Development that can be used to meet protection goals. While its main focus is nutrition for adolescent girls, the scheme provides platform for raising protection concerns with this age group and empowering them with information, knowledge and skills to be able to protect themselves. The Rajiv Gandhi National Scheme for the Children of Working Mothers, implemented by the Ministry of Women and Child Development, is primarily seen as fulfilling child development goals only. However, protection needs of children aged 0-6 years are also met through crèche and day care facilities and hence it may well be taken as a child protection scheme also. There are some schemes for the disabled persons under the Ministry of Social Justice and Empowerment. Since they do not have a child focus or specific component for children, issues of disabled children get very little attention.

8

Women Issues in India: Current Perspective

Women's are the wealth of India and they have contributed in almost every field and made country feel proud at every occasion. They are in front, leading the country, making mile stones and source of inspiration for many. In politics, President Pratibha Patil, Lok Sabha Speaker Meira Kumar, UPA Chairperson Sonia Gandhi, Chief Minister of UP Mayawati and Delhi Sheila Dixit, bureaucracy, Nirupama Roy, in socio-cultural field, Medha Patekar, Arundhati Roy, Shobna Narayanan, Lata Mangeskar, Anjolie Ela Menon, Rekha, Meera Nayar and many others, in sports, Sania Mirja, Saina Nehwal are some of the names at the top.

Women's are also playing important role in national growth and economic development through corporate houses. They are not only working at grass root level but participating in decision making.

Jyoti Naik, President of Lijjat Papad, Kiran Mazumdar, Chairman and Managing Director of Biocon, Naina Lal Kidwai, Deputy CEO of HSBC, Ranjana Kumar, Chairman of NABARD, Ritu Kumar, CEO of Escolife, Priya Paul, Chairman of Apeejay Park Hotels, Indira Nooyi, Chairperson & CEO of Pepsico, Roshani Nadar, CEO of HCL are some of the pioneers in their respective field. At present women's are contributing and participating in every sphere, politics, business, education, science and technology, media, sports, art and culture etc.

However this is the one face of coin and on the other side of coin is the hard truth of the Indian society. There is systematic discrimination and neglect from early childhood of women's in India, which could be in terms of inadequate nutrition, denial or limited access to education, health and property rights, child labour and domestic violence. The fear of sexual violence has been a powerful factor in restricting women's behavior and sense of freedom. The struggle against violence is actually the struggle against the unequal distribution of power both physical and economic between the sexes. It is important to address the root cause for the subordinate status of women in the Indian society. Hillary Clinton, US secretary of State, addressing the Delhi University students on 20 July 2009 said that "women's roles and rights are as important as any issue we can list.

Women are the key of economic growth. It's been established through research". Men should perceive women not as subservient being but as empowered individuals who are equal partners. The issues need to be seen in the context of a patriarchal social framework and a value system based on 'son preference', such as the son being responsible for the carrying forward of the family name, support in old age and for performing the last rites. Further, the practice of dowry and the tag of 'Parayadhan' translate into daughters being considered an economic liability. Women's are not only entitled for survival but also to a life with dignity, grace and equal opportunities so that they can grow to their full potential. There is an urgent need to pay attention to the issues that concern this section of population. The focus should be on poverty reduction, gender justice, health, nutrition, sustained awareness of rights and redressal, eradication of social evils etc.

Political Issues

Women's equality in power sharing and active participation in decision making, including decision making in political process at all levels will ensure the achievement of the goal of women empowerment. Government of India through 73 rd and 74 th Constitutional Amendment Acts reserved the one-third of seats in all local elected bodies for women as a sign of political empowerment. Over a million women have actively entered political life in India through the Panchayat Raj institutions. There are many elected women representatives at the village council level. The percentage of women in various levels of political activities in India have risen considerably, however women are still under-represented in governance and decision-making process. T heir power is restricted, as it the men who wield all the authority. Their decisions are often over-ruled by the government machinery. It is crucial to train and give real power to these women leaders so that they can catalyst change in their villages regarding women. In recent years there have been explicit moves to increase women's political participation at top level. However, the Women's reservation bill is a sad story as it is repeatedly being scuttled in the parliament. All this shows that the process of gender equality and women's empowerment still has a long way to go.

Economic Issues

Women professionals in India are facing a range of problems. Women have extensive workload with dual responsibility of profession and household and they have to balance household demands with those of their profession. Development policies and programs of the country tend not to view women as integral to the economic development process. This is reflected in the higher INVESTMENTS in women's reproductive rather than their productive roles, mainly in population programs.

Women are engage in economically productive work and earn incomes though their earnings are generally low. Most of the women work in agricultural sector either as workers, in household farms or as wageworkers. It is precisely livelihood in agriculture that has tended to become more volatile and insecure in recent years and women cultivators have therefore been negatively affected. The government's policies for alleviating poverty have failed to produce any desirable results, as women do not receive appropriate wages for their labour. There is also significant amount of unpaid or non-marketed labour within the household. The increase in gender disparity in wages in the urban areas is also quite marked as it results from the employment of women in different and lower paying activities. They are exploited at various levels. They should be provided with proper wages and work at par with men so that their status can be elevated in society. There is urgent need to improve women's economic status because they are fundamental to the process of economic development of the country.

Social and Cultural Issues

The socio-cultural attributes in society have left a deep mark on women empowerment in India. Parents depend on sons for support in old age and looked to them as potential builders of family prestige and prosperity whereas daughters are considered to destine for others. Women's in India need and expect equal access to education, health, nutrition, employment and productive resources. In fact they are fighting for their rights to decide their own path for development.

Education

The female literacy rate in India is though gradually rising, it's lower than the male. According to the National Survey data (1997), only the states of Kerala and Mizoram have approached universal female literacy rates. The gender gap in education is far greater in northern states of India. Although in states where enrollment rates for girls are higher, many girls drop out of school after a few years of education. Factors such as inhibition on education being imparted by male teachers to girls once they reach puberty, is responsible for drop out. Consequences are that early marriage and child birth pronounced in families of lower socio-economic status.

Health and Nutrition

The socio-cultural practice of women eating last in the family has eminent effect on her health especially if it is a household in low economic status. Most direct effects of poor health and nutrition among women in Indian society are high mortality rates among young children and women of child bearing age. A women health and nutrition status influence her newborn's birth weight and chance of survival. Post neo-natal death is generally caused by infectious diseases. The incidence and severity of most of this disease are affected by controllable factors such as immunization, health care and nutrition. Due to gender biased, these factors are not controlled equally for male and female children. Maternal mortality in India estimated at 437 maternal deaths per 100,000 live births, result primarily from infection hemorrhage, obstructed labour, abortion and anemia.

Crimes against Women

Crimes against women are of various natures. It include crimes involving sexual exploitation for economic gains like prostitution & trafficking, adultery, abduction, rape, wrongful confinement, and murder etc on the one hand and crimes related to women's property like dishonest misappropriation, criminal breach of trust, domestic violence, dowry extortion and outraging the modesty of women etc on the other. These crimes are not only injurious and immoral for the women but for the society as a whole.

Domestic Violence

In Indian society, it is widely accepted that within the family the man is the master and women is the inferior and subordinate partner and societal pressure force women to maintain this status quo. Wife beating is the most prevalent form of violence against women in the Indian society and it is viewed as a general problem of domestic discord. According to National Crime Report Bureau, 1.5 lakh crimes against women are registered annually out of which nearly 50,000 are related to domestic violence in their homes.

Female Infanticide and Feticide

This is playing a significant role in lop sided sex ratio in India. Poor families in certain regions of the country sometimes resort to killing baby girls at birth, to avoid an unwanted burden on family resources. Sex selective abortion has also been common in the country. It's dangerous to abort the foetus after 18 weeks of pregnancy and quiet harmful for mother too at such a late stage. Various techniques of sex determination and sex pre-selection have been discovered during the last fifteen years, such as sonography, fetoscopy, needling, chorion biopsy and the most popular amniocentesis have increasingly become household names in India. Amniocentesis technique is used in the small town and also in some cities of states like Gujrat, Maharashtra, Uttar Pradesh, Bihar, Madhya Pradesh, Punjab, Tamilnadu, Rajasthan etc. Mumbai and Delhi are also the major center for sex determination and sex pre-selection tests.

Dowry

Dowry remains the major reason for discrimination and injustice towards women in India. When dowry demands are not met, it precipitates into serious consequence for the young bride. The Dowry Prohibition Act of 1961 marks the first attempt by the Government of India to recognize dowry as a social evil and to curb its practice. The act was modified with the Dowry Prohibition Amendment Act of 1984, which has again been modified with Dowry Prohibition Bill 1986. Women's organization have played key role in this process of change. The 1961 Act define dowry and makes the practice of dowry- giving and taking, a punishable offence. However, i t is ridiculous to see that even among highly educated sections, the articles of dowry are proudly exhibited in the marriage as a status symbol. The dowry abuse is increasing in India. The most severe is 'bride burning', the burning of women whose dowries were not considered sufficient by their husband or in-laws. Most of these incidents are reported as accidental burns in the kitchen or are disguised as suicide. Dowry is one of those social evils that no educated woman will own up with pride, still many are adhering to it. Practices of dowry tend to subordinate women in the society. Women should be more economically empowered and should be educated properly regarding the various legal provisions such as Section 498A CrPC, protection from domestic violence etc., only then this evil menace could possibly be eradicated from Indian social system.

Rape

Rape is the fastest growing crime in India compared to murder, robbery and kidnapping. According to the report of National Crime Records Bureau (NCRB), every 60 minutes, two women are raped in this country. A total of 20,737 cases of rape were reported in the year 2007, registering a 7.2 percent increase over the previous year. According to NCRB, 19,348 rape cases were reported in the year 2006. The biggest number of such crimes was reported from Madhya Pradesh. One-quarter of the victims were minors, 75 percent of culprits were known to victims and 10 percent were relatives.

These figures are underestimations as many incidents go unreported due to fear of stigma and non awareness of rights. There are also the countless cases of eve teasing, indecent gazes, pinching, brushes and comments that infringe upon the rights of women, especially in overcrowded spaces and public transport buses and trains.

Major cities in the country have become the hub of misdemeanor because of technological reach. Mobile, cyber café, car, beach, mall, restaurant, hotel have become popular apparatus for the criminals. What precipitates the problem is that the incidents of rape, sexual molestation and harassment have been followed by dubious attempts by perpetrators and law enforcers to arm-twist the course of justice. There is a need for a drastic change in attitudes and mindsets towards such incidents. Poor investigations, harsh cross examination of victims, senseless adjournment of cases and faulty assessment of evidence and furnishing of evidence by victims in presence of culprits are areas that need reforms.

In the year 2007 for which the latest data is available from the National Crime Records Bureau, seven of the ten fastest rising crimes in India were those against women. While the incidence of all cognizable crimes under the Indian Penal code rose by under 5 percent over the previous year, dowry deaths registered an increase of 15 percent, cruelty by husband and relatives 14 percent, kidnapping and abduction of females 13 percent, importation of girls 12 percent and sexual harassment by 11 percent.

Rape and molestation cases grew by a more modest 6-7 percent, but even that was higher than the average rate. Despite the increasing cases of crime against women, they would appear to be not in priority list of the investigating agencies. The NCRB data shows that investigation starts within the same year in only one out of 10 sexual harassment cases and only two out of ten cases of molestation or cruelty by husband and relatives. Similarly, only three out of ten rapes and dowry deaths are investigated within the same year.

A comparative study of the data available about these crimes suggest that there were rise in the crimes against women in 2008 compared to the previous year. While a total of 1,012 cases were registered for kidnap of women in 2007, the number went up to 1,494 in 2008.

Similarly, the number of incidents related to dowry death rose from 1,226 in 2007 to 1,233 in 2008. Similarly, cases of atrocities perpetrated for dowry rose to 2,230 in 2008 from 1,493 in 2007. Cases related to eve-teasing and molestation shot up to 188 during 2008, 20 more than those recorded in the previous year. Also incidents related to kidnapping of women increased from 1,012 in 2007 to 1,494 in 2008. The fact remains that there is sufficient information about crime against women that calls for appropriate remedial actions.

THE CRITICAL CONDITION OF WOMEN IN RURAL INDIA

Uttarakhand women have always emerged as the pillars of the rural economy due to their total involvement with agriculture, forest protection, cattle care and dairying. The male members of the family usually migrate to towns to earn a living for their families. Thus, women in villages become the heads of the family. Even where the men continue to reside in the villages, it is the women and girls who look after the agriculture and cattle.

Typically the leftover food is meagre, considering the families are poor and have little to begin with. This creates a major problem with malnutrition, especially for pregnant or nursing women. Few women seek medical care while pregnant because it is thought of as a temporary condition. This is one main reason why India's maternal and infant mortality rates are so high.

Starting from birth, girls do not receive as much care and commitment from their parents and society as a boy would. For example, a new baby girl would only be breast fed for a short period of time, barely supplying her with the nutrients she needs.

This is so that the mother can get pregnant as soon as possible, in hopes of a son the next time.

Uttarakhand women have been the backbone of the State's economy. They have always stood in the forefront during the struggle of State formation. Women are the mainstay of the culture and traditions of the hills. Repeatedly, hill women have shown remarkable courage and participation in development programs. The life in the hilly areas of Uttarakhand is very difficult. Despite the adverse conditions, the rural women of the area portrayed immense potential and prominence in the society. Almost all the women in the society are employed in one way or other. In some cases their status was better off than any woman living in a hi-tech city or metro like Delhi. A woman in Uttarakhand is earning Rs. 18.13 per day. This is more than the per capita income of India. But the potential of Uttarakhand women is still not being utilized fully. Thus, there is a need to raise the status and standard of women in Uttarakhand. Women who are working on the farm were suffering form a lot of problems. They are major contributors in the inside activities as well as outside activities. There is a need to assess the socio-economic status of the farm women.

The Condition of Hilly Women

Women are the centres of the family. Though the role of women is very important and crucial in a hill economy, yet they are the invisible workers and lead a tough life. Women are actively engaged in all the activities right from the house to the fields.Â Â Interaction among women takes place during their work in the field and /or forest, kitchen, during washing clothes etc. sometimes they make courtesy visits to their neighbours. There is no strict *parda* (veil) system in the village. Women are free to move for marketing and other household activities but they have to cover their head with their *saree* as a token of respect to the elders.

During my visit to *Dogra* village in the Nainital distict of Uttarakhand, I observed many social taboos among the hilly women. The very first social taboo is reflected during the period of menstruation. During this, women are not allowed or they themselves do not enter into the kitchen or place of worship inside or outside the house. They sit at a distance and sleep on a blanket laid on the ground during this period. After three days they wash their hair and take a 'complete bath'. They wash their used blankets, bed sheets and clothes after five days. This is done outside the house and near a natural water stream. They do not touch food items like pickle or even plants bearing fruits. It is said that if touched, the fruits will become rotten. If someone within or outside the family touches the body by chance, he/she has to be sprinkled with *Gangajal*/cow's urine/water touched with gold ornament. Only then can the person enter inside the house. During these five days, either the husband or other women in the family does cooking. But the women can go for farm/forest for work. Women lead even tougher lives during the winter. This practice is not as commonly-practiced in urban or semi-urban societies these days. The women face many other problems due to the rigid conduct that is expected of them with respect to familial roles—

Health Problems

Lack of Knowledge about Dietary Pattern: Nutrition requirement depends on the age and sex of an individual. Women have a lack of knowledge about the dietary pattern best suited to different age groups. They do not know how much food they need to consume during the time of pregnancy and about the lactation period for women. Lack of knowledge thus is a cause of high maternal mortality rate among the women. They suffer from various health problems such as anaemia, weakness and vomiting.

Gender disparities: Gender has been the most statistically significant determinant of malnutrition among young children, and malnutrition is a frequent direct or underlying cause of death among girls below the age of five. It was also found that women use to eat whatever was left after feeding it to the male members of the family. Women also used to consuming the leftover meals of the day for dinner. Girls were breast-fed less frequently and for shorter durations during infancy and childhood and during adulthood, while males were fed first and better.

Infectious Diseases: It was found that improper disposal of waste and working barefoot leads to high instances of hookworm infection in rural areas. Hookworm infection is directly responsible for a high percentage of anaemia among women.

Medical Amenities: Uttarakhand is a newly formed state with Government health services still in the process of formation. In the area surveyed, there was one hospital which had two lady doctors. One was an eye specialist and the other was dealing with all other health problems concerning women. According to the women they have limited knowledge and took little interest in their patients. Doctors are in clinic very erratically, and women suffered a lot as a result of this.

Lack of Nutritional Education: It was found that women have low level of Nutritional education. Low nutrition education explains the poor intake of vitamin rich food; especially green vegetables among women, even though they are available in plenty in the Pantnagar area.

Lack of Knowledge of Human Rights

Child Labour- A considerable amount of girl children are employed in strenuous activities.Â They lack awareness about the Child Labour Act and its protectionary measures to prevent it.

Women's Rights — Women, constituting the weaker section of the society, are suffering from various problems in every field. Today, the government has initiated various programmes related to Anti-dowry and maternal benefits, but women lack awareness about these laws and rules. The two women who wereÂ working in the Pantnagar field had no men to support them in household activities, and many women were also on the receiving end of various forms of violence from their male counterparts.

Agriculture Policies- Agriculture, being the backbone of most of the rural population needs particular attention from both, our planners and purveyors of knowledge. Government has initiated various policies and laws in Agriculture. Even though they live near the Agriculture University of Pantnagar, women had no idea about the services they could access, including the toll-free helpline.

The above findings only go on to prove that the difficulties faced by women are two-fold. As women in developing countries move into the work force, their domestic responsibilities are not alleviated. Women work two full-time jobs. One, in a Pantnagar farm where they are paid, the second is in the home where they are paid nothing. Women are not educated and cannot hold a prestigious job, and as a result, they take on the most physically difficult and undesirable jobs. A typical day for a woman in an agricultural labour force lasts from 8am to 5pm, with only an hour break in the middle. Most women are overworked, with no maternity leave or special breaks. They have insufficient knowledge about a balanced diet and most of the females were unhealthy due to gender discrimination. As India is male-dominated society, all the decision is taken by the male members in the family. Women, as 'invisible workers' contribute a lot to household activities as well as other outer activities. Agriculture is the backbone of Indian farming. Women, though equally engaged in farming activities, lack knowledge of agriculture policies and services, and other social benefits.

WOMEN RIGHTS IN INDIA: CONSTITUTIONAL RIGHTS AND LEGAL RIGHTS

Constitutional Rights to Women:

The rights and safeguards enshrined in the constitution for women in India are listed below:

1. The state shall not discriminate against any citizen of India on the ground of sex [Article 15(1)].
2. The state is empowered to make any special provision for women. In other words, this provision enables the state to make affirmative discrimination in favour of women [Article 15(3)].
3. No citizen shall be discriminated against or be ineligible for any employment or office under the state on the ground of sex [Article 16(2)].
4. Traffic in human beings and forced labour are prohibited [Article 23(1)].
5. The state to secure for men and women equally the right to an adequate means of livelihood [Article 39(a)].

6. The state to secure equal pay for equal work for both Indian men and women [Article 39(d)].
7. The state is required to ensure that the health and strength of women workers are not abused and that they are not forced by economic necessity to enter avocations unsuited to their strength [Article 39(e)].
8. The state shall make provision for securing just and humane conditions of work and maternity relief [Article 42].
9. It shall be the duty of every citizen of India to renounce practices derogatory to the dignity of women [Article 51-A(e)].
10. One-third of the total number of seats to be filled by direct election in every Panchayat shall be reserved for women [Article 243-D(3)].
11. One-third of the total number of offices of chairpersons in the Panchayats at each level shall be reserved for women [Article 243-D(4)].
12. One-third of the total number of seats to be filled by direct election in every Municipality shall be reserved for women [Article 243-T(3)].
13. The offices of chairpersons in the Municipalities shall be reserved for women in such manner as the State Legislature may provide [Article 243-T(4)].

Legal Rights to Women:

The following various legislation's contain several rights and safeguards for women:

1. Protection of Women from Domestic Violence Act (2005) is a comprehensive legislation to protect women in India from all forms of domestic violence. It also covers women who have been/are in a relationship with the abuser and are subjected to violence of any kind—physical, sexual, mental, verbal or emotional.
2. Immoral Traffic (Prevention) Act (1956) is the premier legislation for prevention of trafficking for commercial sexual exploitation. In other words, it prevents trafficking

in women and girls for the purpose of prostitution as an organised means of living.

3. Indecent Representation of Women (Prohibition) Act (1986) prohibits indecent representation of women through advertisements or in publications, writings, paintings, figures or in any other manner.
4. Commission of Sati (Prevention) Act (1987) provides for the more effective prevention of the commission of sati and its glorification on women.
5. Dowry Prohibition Act (1961) prohibits the giving or taking of dowry at or before or any time after the marriage from women.
6. Maternity Benefit Act (1961) regulates the employment of women in certain establishments for certain period before and after child-birth and provides for maternity benefit and certain other benefits.
7. Medical Termination of Pregnancy Act (1971) provides for the termination of certain pregnancies by registered medical practitioners on humanitarian and medical grounds.
8. Pre-Conception and Pre-Natal Diagnostic Techniques (Prohibition of Sex Selection) Act (1994) prohibits sex selection before or after conception and prevents the misuse of pre-natal diagnostic techniques for sex determination leading to female foeticide.
9. Equal Remuneration Act (1976) provides for payment of equal remuneration to both men and women workers for same work or work of a similar nature. It also prevents discrimination on the ground of sex, against women in recruitment and service conditions.
10. Dissolution of Muslim Marriages Act (1939) grants a Muslim wife the right to seek the dissolution of her marriage.
11. Muslim Women (Protection of Rights on Divorce) Act (1986) protects the rights of Muslim women who have been divorced by or have obtained divorce from their husbands.

12. Family Courts Act (1984) provides for the establishment of Family Courts for speedy settlement of family disputes.
13. Indian Penal Code (1860) contains provisions to protect Indian women from dowry death, rape, kidnapping, cruelty and other offences.
14. Code of Criminal Procedure (1973) has certain safeguards for women like obligation of a person to maintain his wife, arrest of woman by female police and so on.
15. Indian Christian Marriage Act (1872) contain provisions relating to marriage and divorce among the Christian community.
16. Legal Services Authorities Act (1987) provides for free legal services to Indian women.
17. Hindu Marriage Act (1955) introduced monogamy and allowed divorce on certain specified grounds. It provided equal rights to Indian man and woman in respect of marriage and divorce.
18. Hindu Succession Act (1956) recognizes the right of women to inherit parental property equally with men.
19. Minimum Wages Act (1948) does not allow discrimination between male and female workers or different minimum wages for them.
20. Mines Act (1952) and Factories Act (1948) prohibits the employment of women between 7 P.M. to 6 A.M. in mines and factories and provides for their safety and welfare.
21. The following other legislation's also contain certain rights and safeguards for women:
    1. Employees' State Insurance Act (1948)
    2. Plantation Labour Act (1951)
    3. Bonded Labour System (Abolition) Act (1976)
    4. Legal Practitioners (Women) Act (1923)
    5. Indian Succession Act (1925)
    6. Indian Divorce Act (1869)
    7. Parsi Marriage and Divorce Act (1936)

8. Special Marriage Act (1954)
9. Foreign Marriage Act (1969)
10. Indian Evidence Act (1872)
11. Hindu Adoptions and Maintenance Act (1956).

22. National Commission for Women Act (1990) provided for the establishment of a National Commission for Women to study and monitor all matters relating to the constitutional and legal rights and safeguards of women.
23. Sexual Harassment of Women at Workplace (Prevention, Prohibition and Redressal). Act (2013) provides protection to women from sexual harassment at all workplaces both in public and private sector, whether organised or unorganized.

WOMEN IN INDIA & HUMAN RIGHTS

What ever discussion goes on, the bottom line is there are no human rights for the women in India, absolutely none. She is lucky if she doesnï¿½t get exploited, abused etc. Shear luck, because if at all that happens no one will help her not even her own family (May be they are involved too in this). So if any of you have a daughter just pray to god that she is lucky enough to live a human life. Even if a girl is raped in our society, no matter how bold she is, she never goes to legal process. The reason is:

1. There is no term as legal process in India.
2. She is so repressed for her future that she thinks keeping quite will not expose her to the society.
3. She never ever will have courage to fight against the criminal herself.

This is so scary that thinking of living in this system will scare the hell out of the western country citizens. In other words any person can do anything to women without any hesitation and he can still enjoy his life. May be there are too many article on women exploitation and we have all heard them so much that we hardly care any more.

Think of the same happening to your own little children, we get agitated if someone beats our children, even if it is for a reason.

And now apply that to the women who are weaker section of the society. They need protection form men around them. If not they are better of living in a jungle. I think for women in India I have only one sentence.

The human being is not yet civilized and they are still living in the forest where there is a danger of wild animals attacking them any timeï¿½. May be forest is safer than India for women. I am ashamed myself to be part of this country where we cannot even give a safe future to our women and children. Unlike other countries who spare their lives for giving great future to their generation.

Violence Against Women: A Fact Sheet

In the US, a woman is raped every 6 minutes; a woman is battered every 15 seconds. In North Africa, 6,000 women are genitally mutilated each day. This year, more than 15,000 women will be sold into sexual slavery in China. 200 women in Bangladesh will be horribly disfigured when their spurned husbands or suitors burn them with acid.

More than 7,000 women in India will be murdered by their families and in-laws in disputes over dowries. Violence against women is rooted in a global culture of discrimination which denies women equal rights with men and which legitimizes the appropriation of women's bodies for individual gratification or political ends.

Every year, violence in the home and the community devastates the lives of millions of women. (*Broken Bodies, Shattered Minds: Torture and Ill Treatment of Women, Amnesty International, 2001*)

Stop Violence Against Women!

Violence against women is a violation of human rights that cannot be justified by any political, religious, or cultural claim. A global culture of discrimination against women allows violence to occur daily and with impunity. Amnesty International calls on you to help us eradicate violence against women and help women to achieve lives of equality and human dignity.

Background

- Violence against women feeds off discrimination and serves to reinforce it. When women are abused in custody, when they are raped by armed forces as "spoils of war", or when they are terrorized by violence in the home, unequal power relations between men and women are both manifested and enforced.
- Violence against women is compounded by discrimination on the grounds of race, ethnicity, sexual identity, social status, class, and age. Such multiple forms of discrimination further restrict women's choices, increase their vulnerability to violence and make it even harder for women to obtain justice.
- There is an unbroken spectrum of violence that women face at the hands of people who exert control over them. States have the obligation to prevent, protect against, and punish violence against women whether perpetrated by private or public actors. States have a responsibility to uphold standards of due diligence and take steps to fulfill their responsibility to protect individuals from human rights abuses.

International Women's Human Rights Foundations

- *The Universal Declaration of Human Rights* states that "everyone is entitled to all the rights and freedoms set forth in this Declaration, without distinction of any kind, such as race, color, sex, language, religion, political or other opinion, national or social origin, property, birth or other status." (Article 2)
- *The Declaration on the Elimination of Violence Against Women* states that "violence against women means any act of gender-based violence that results in, or is likely to result in, physical, sexual or psychological harm or suffering to women, including threats of such acts, coercion or arbitrary deprivation of liberty, whether occurring in public or in private life." (Article 1) It further asserts that states have an obligation to " exercise due diligence to prevent,

investigate and, in accordance with national legislation, punish acts of violence against women, whether those acts are perpetrated by the State or by private persons." (Article 4-c)

- *The Convention on the Elimination of all forms of Discrimination Against Women (CEDAW)*, defines discrimination against women as any "distinction, exclusion or restriction made on the basis of sex which has the effect or purpose of impairing or nullifying the recognition, enjoyment or exercise by women, irrespective of their marital status, on the basis of equality between men and women, of human rights or fundamental freedoms in the political, economic, social, cultural, civil or any other field." (Article 1)

Violence Against Women: A Human Rights Violation

Violence against women is rampant in all corners of the world. Such violence is a human rights violation that manifests itself in a number of ways, including:

Violence against Women in Custody

The imbalance of power between inmates and guards is a result of prisoners' total dependency on correctional officers and guards' ability to withhold privileges and is manifest in direct physical force and indirect abuses. Because incarcerated women are largely invisible to the public eye, little is done when the punishment of imprisonment is compounded with that of rape, sexual assault, groping during body searches, and shackling during childbirth. Women are often coerced into providing sex for "favors" such as extra food or personal hygiene products, or to avoid punishment. There is little medical or psychological care available to inmates. Though crimes in prison such as rape are prevalent, few perpetrators of violence against female inmates are ever held accountable. In 1997, for example, only ten prison employees in the entire federal system were disciplined for sexual misconduct.

Acid Burning and Dowry Deaths

Women's subjugation to men is pervasive in the political, civil, social, cultural, and economic spheres of many countries. In such societies, a woman who turns down a suitor or does not get along with her in-laws far too frequently becomes a victim of a violent form of revenge: acid burning. Acid is thrown in her face or on her body and can blind her in addition to often fatal third-degree burns. Governments do little to prevent the sale of acid to the public or to punish those who use it to kill and maim. Similarly, the ongoing reality of dowry-related violence is an example of what can happen when women are treated as property. Brides unable to pay the high "price" to marry are punished by violence and often death at the hands of their in-laws or their own husbands.

"Honor" Killings

In some societies, women are often looked upon as representatives of the honor of the family. When women are suspected of extra-marital sexual relations, even if in the case of rape, they can be subjected to the cruelest forms of indignity and violence, often by their own fathers or brothers. Women who are raped and are unable to provide explicit evidence, are sometimes accused of zina, or the crime of unlawful sexual relations, the punishment for which is often death by public stoning. Such laws serve as a great obstacle inhibiting women from pursuing cases against those who raped them. Assuming an accused woman's guilt, male family members believe that they have no other means of undoing a perceived infringement of "honor" other than to kill the woman.

Domestic Violence

Violence against women is a global pandemic. Without exception, a woman's greatest risk of violence is from someone she knows. Domestic violence is a violation of a woman's right to physical integrity, to liberty, and all too often, to her right to life itself. When states fail to take the basic steps needed to protect women from domestic violence or allow these crimes to be committed with impunity, states are failing in their obligation to protect women from torture.

Female Genital Mutilation

Female genital mutilation is the removal of part or all of the external female genitalia. In its most severe form, a woman or girl has all of her genitalia removed and then stitched together, leaving a small opening for intercourse and menstruation. It is practiced in 28 African countries on the pretext of cultural tradition or hygiene. An estimated 135 million girls have undergone FGM with dire consequences ranging from infection (including HIV) to sterility, in addition to the devastating psychological effects. Though all the governments of the countries in which FGM is practiced have legislation making it illegal, the complete lack of enforcement and prosecution of the perpetrators means FGM continues to thrive.

Perceived Sexual Identity

Sexuality is regulated in a gender specific way and maintained through strict constraints imposed by cultural norms and sometimes through particular legal measures supporting those norms. The community, which can include religious institutions, the media, family and cultural networks, regulates women's sexuality and punishes women who do not comply. Such women include lesbians, women who appear "too masculine," women who try to freely exercise their rights, and women who challenge male dominance.

Lesbian women, or women who are perceived to be lesbian, experience abuses by state authorities in prisons, by the police, as well as private actors such as their family and community. Numerous cases document young lesbians being beaten, raped, forcibly impregnated or married, and otherwise attacked by family members to punish them or "correct" their sexual identity. Lesbians in the United States face well-founded fears of persecution by police because of their sexual identity and violence against lesbians occurs with impunity on a regular basis.

Gender Based Asylum

The UN High Commission on Refugees advocates that "women fearing persecution or severe discrimination on the basis of their gender should be considered a member of a social group for the purposes of determining refugee status." (*Guidelines on the Protection of Refugee Women*) Such persecution may include harms unique to their gender such as, but not limited to, female genital mutilation, forcible abortion, domestic violence that the state refuses to act on and honor killings. However, women seeking asylum in the United States rarely gain refugee status based on claims of gender-related violence, as U.S. asylum adjudicators apply a restrictive interpretation of the international definition of a refugee entitled to persecution. In particular, lesbian women seeking asylum from sexuality-based persecution in their countries of origin often, and legitimately, fear disclosing their sexuality to authorities.

CONSTITUTIONAL RIGHTS FOR WOMEN IN INDIA

The Constitution of India guarantees equality of sexes and in fact grants special favours to women. These can be found in three articles of the Constitution. Article 14 says that the government shall not deny to any person equality before law or the equal protection of the laws. Article 15 declares that government shall not discriminate against any citizen on the ground of sex. Article 15 (3) makes a special provision enabling the State to make affirmative discriminations in favour of women. Moreover, the government can pass special laws in favour of women. Article 16 guarantees that no citizen shall be discriminated against in matters of public employment on the grounds of sex. Article 42 directs the State to make provision for ensuring just and humane conditions of work and maternity relief. The Constitution imposes a fundamental duty on every citizen through Articles 15 (A) (e) to renounce the practices derogatory to the dignity of women.

All these are fundamental rights. Therefore, a woman can go to the court if one is subjected to any discrimination. When we talk about constitutional rights of women in India, we mainly pertain to those areas where discrimination is done against women and special laws formulated to fight those bigotries. The most important issues stand as those pertaining to marriage, children, abortion, crimes against women, and inheritance.

Before modern Hindu laws were passed, child marriages were the norms, inter-caste marriages were banned, the girl became a part of the husband's family, and polygamy was common. In the 19th century, the British rulers passed several laws to protect customs and traditions while abolishing detestable practices like Sati. Some such revolutionary laws were Hindu Widows Remarriage Act 1865 and the Brahmo Samaj Marriage Act 1872, the forerunner of the present Special Marriage Act. In the beginning, the Act sets four essential conditions for a valid Hindu marriage.

They are:

- Monogamy
- Sound mind
- Marriageable age
- The parties should not be too closely related.

Polygamy was permitted among Hindus before the Act was passed in 1955. However, after the act was passed, any man marrying again while his wife is living will be punished with fine and imprisonment up to seven years. Formerly, child marriages were common. The Child Marriage Act of 1929 was not very effective as such marriages were continued to be performed. Now, however, the bridegroom must be 21 years old and the bride 18 years. However, there is a separate Muslim Code of Conduct, which allows polygamy of up to four wives as per Islamic laws. A marriage may be invalid without the boy or the girl realizing it at the time of the wedding. A civil marriage would be void if four essential conditions are not complied with.

These conditions are listed in the Special Marriage Act as enumerated below:

- If it is bigamy
- If either party was suffering from mental disorder
- If the boy has not completed 21 years and the girl 18 years
- The boy and the girl are too closely related, or in legal language, are "within degrees of prohibited relationship" unless custom governing at least one party permits the marriage between them. Prohibited relationships are listed in he Special Marriage Act.
- A fifth reason for invalidating a marriage is impotence of either party.

There are some grounds available to the wife only, both in Hindu and civil marriages. One such ground available exclusively to the wife is her husband's commission of rape, sodomy or bestiality. Under the Hindu Adoptions and Maintenance Act 1956, a Hindu wife is entitled to be maintained by her husband.

Section 125 of the Criminal Procedure Code also deals with maintenance of wife and children. If there is a decree of maintenance against the husband and the couple have been living apart for over one year, it would be a ground for the wife to seek dissolution of marriage. Here again the Muslim Personal Law has a different set of conditions for the annulment of an Islamic marriage.

The Dowry Prohibition Act of 1961 says that any person who gives, takes, or abets the giving or taking of dowry shall be punished with imprisonment, which may extend to six months or with fine up to Rs. 5,000 or with both. Dowry that started off as a practice to give away presents to the departing daughter, usually some resources to begin her new married life, slowly assumed extraordinary proportions and turned into a social evil. Brides were expected to bring the "gifts" regardless of their personal willingness. The bride's family could no longer have an individual say; lists were prepared and sent to the girl's house before the final agreement between the two families. The condition being that the boy would marry the girl only if the demands were met. Such a custom is being practiced not only in India but also in other countries like Bangladesh and Nepal. The reason behind this custom is the poor economical condition of the people along with a lack of education; unawareness of legal rights among women and a general bias against the women.

Crimes like rape, kidnapping, eve teasing and indecent exposure can be grouped as crimes against women. Rape is the worst crime against women after murder and the maximum punishment under the Indian Penal Code (IPC) is life imprisonment. An abortion or miscarriage due to natural causes is not an offence. Therefore, the law does not deal with it. However, violent and forceful abortion is a crime. Sections 312 and 316 of the Indian Penal Code deal with abortion as crime. Section 313 deals with abortion without the consent of the woman. The punishment could even be life imprisonment. The Hindu Succession Act gives male and female heirs almost equal right to inheritance. Section 14 says that any property possessed by a female Hindu shall be held by her as full owner and not as a limited owner.

MODERN INDIAN WOMEN

The status of women in modern India is a sort of a paradox. If on one hand she is at the peak of ladder of success, on the other hand she is mutely suffering the violence afflicted on her by her own family members. As compared with past women in modern times have achieved a lot but in reality they have to still travel a long way. Their path is full of roadblocks. The women have left the secured domain of their home and are now in the battlefield of life, fully armored with their talent. They had proven themselves. But in India they are yet to get their dues. The sex ratio of India shows that the Indian society is still prejudiced against female. There are 933 females per thousand males in India according to the census of 2001, which is much below the world average of 990 females. There are many problems which women in India have to go through daily. These problems have become the part and parcel of life of Indian women and some of them have accepted them as their fate.

The main problems of Indian women includes:

Malnutrition

Generally in India, women are the one who eat last and least in the whole family. So they eat whatever is left after men folk are satiated. As a result most of the times their food intake does not contain the nutritional value required in maintaining the healthy body. In villages, sometimes women do not get to eat the whole meal due to poverty. The UNICEF report of 1996 clearly states that the women of South Asia are not given proper care, which results in higher level of malnutrition among the women of South Asia than anywhere else in the world. This nutritional deficiency has two major consequences for women first they become anemic and second they never achieve their full growth, which leads to an unending cycle of undergrowth as malnourished women cannot give birth to a healthy baby.

Lack of education

In India women education never got its due share of attention. From the medieval India women were debarred from the educational field. According to medieval perception women need just household education and this perception of medieval India still persists in villages of India even today. Girls are supposed to fulfill domestic duties and education becomes secondary for them whereas it is considered to be important for boys. Although scenario in urban areas has changed a lot and women are opting for higher education but majority of Indian population residing in villages still live in medieval times. The people of villages consider girls to be curse and they do not want to waste money and time on them as they think that women should be wedded off as soon as possible.

The main reason for not sending girls to school is the poor economic condition. Another reason is far off location of schools. In Indian society virginity and purity is given utmost importance during marriage and people are afraid to send their girl child to far off schools were male teacher teach them along with boys.

The lack of education is the root cause for many other problems. An uneducated mother cannot look after her children properly and she is not aware of the deadly diseases and their cure, which leads to the poor health of the children. An uneducated person does not know about hygiene this lack of knowledge of hygiene may lead to poor health of the whole family.

Female infanticide/foeticide

As women were supposed to be and in some areas of India are still considered to be curse by some strata of society their birth was taken as a burden. So in past times they were killed as soon as they were born. In some of the Rajput clans of Rajasthan newly born girl child was dropped in a large bowl of milk and was killed. Today with the help of technology the sex of the unborn baby is determined and if it is a girl child then it is aborted down. In all this procedure women do not have any say they have to do according to the wish of their husbands even if she does not wan to abort she have any choice.

Divorce

The divorce rate in India is not so high compared to western countries but it does not mean that marriages are more successful here. The reason behind low level of divorce rate is that it is looked down by the society. It is regarded as the sign of failure of marriage, especially of women. She is treated as if she has committed some crime by divorcing her husband. In some communities like Muslims women did not have the right to divorce their husband they were divorced at just the pronouncement of " I divorce you" by their husband thrice and they could not do anything except to be the mute spectator. Recently Muslim Law Board has given right of divorce to women. After divorce women is entitled to get her "Mehar" for herself and her children's sustenance. In Hindu society women get maintenance for themselves and their children after divorce.

Dowry

In 1961, the Government of India passed the Dowry Prohibition Act, making the dowry demands in wedding arrangements illegal. However, many cases of dowry-related domestic violence, suicides and murders have been reported. In the 1980s, numerous such cases were reported.

In 1985, the Dowry Prohibition (maintenance of lists of presents to the bride and bridegroom) rules were framed. According to these rules, a signed list of presents given at the time of the marriage to the bride and the bridegroom should be maintained. The list should contain a brief description of each present, its approximate value, the name of whoever has given the present and his/her relationship to the person. However, such rules are hardly enforced.

A 1997 report claimed that at least 5,000 women die each year because of dowry deaths, and at least a dozen die each day in 'kitchen fires' thought to be intentional. The term for this is "bride burning" and is criticized within India itself. Amongst the urban educated, such dowry abuse has reduced considerably.

Land and property rights

In most Indian families , women do not own any property in their own names, and do not get a share of parental property. Due to weak enforcement of laws protecting them, women continue to have little access to land and property. In fact, some of the laws discriminate against women, when it comes to land and property rights. The Hindu personal laws of mid-1956s (applied to Hindus, Buddhists, Sikhs and Jains) gave women rights to inheritance. However, the sons had an independent share in the ancestral property, while the daughters' shares were based on the share received by their father.

Hence, a father could effectively disinherit a daughter by renouncing his share of the ancestral property, but the son will continue to have a share in his own right. Additionally, married daughters, even those facing marital harassment, had no residential rights in the ancestral home. After amendment of Hindu laws in 2005, now women in have been provided the same status as that of men.

In 1986, the Supreme Court of India ruled that Shah Bano, an old divorced Muslim woman was eligible for maintenance money. However, the decision was vociferously opposed by fundamentalist Muslim leaders, who alleged that the court was interfering in their personal law. The Union Government subsequently passed the Muslim Women's (Protection of Rights Upon Divorce) Act. Similarly, the Christian women have struggled over years for equal rights of divorce and succession. In 1994, all the churches, jointly with women's organisations, drew up a draft law called the Christian Marriage and Matrimonial Causes Bill. However, the government has still not amended the relevant laws.

Bibliography

Barnes, D.: *From Communication to Curriculum,* London, Pelican, 1990.

Bentley, T. : *Learning beyond the Classroom: Education for a Changing World,* London, Routledge. 1998.

Bhatia, S.C.: *Education and Social Cultural Disadvance,* Delhi Xeres Publication, 1982.

Brock-Utne, Birgit: *Women, Education and Development,* Oslo, University of Oslo, 1990.

Burnaford, G.: *Teachers Doing Research,* Mahwah, Lawrence Erlbaum.

Chumbow, B.S. : *The Place of Mother Tongue in the National Policy of Educational Guidance,* Port Harcourt, Nigeria, 1990.

Cohen, B.: *Deviant Street Networks: Prostitution in New York City,* Lexington, MA: Lexington Books, 1980.

Cook, Rachel, *Surrogate Motherhood: International Perspective,* Hart Publishing, New York (2003)

Diller, D.: *Literacy Work Stations: Making Centers Work,* Portland, Stenhouse, 2003.

Donoghue, M.: *Foreign Language and the Elementary School Child,* Dubuque, William C. Brown, 1968.

Elliott, J. : *Action Research for Educational Change,* Milton Keynes, Open University, 1991.

Emmerson, Glenda, *Surrogacy: Born for Another, Queensland Parliamentary Library: Publication and Resource Sections,* Brisbane (1996)

Erminio, Peter Volpe, *Test-tube Conception: A Blend of Love and Science,* Mercer University Press, Georgia, USA (1987)

Field, Martha A., *Surrogate Motherhood: The Legal and Human Issues,* Harvard University Press, London (1990)

Fisher, Michael : *A Clash of Cultures: Awadh the British, and the Mughals,* New Delhi, Manohar, 1987.

Fleenor, Juliann: *The Female Gothic.* London: Eden Press, 1983.

Galbraith, M.W. : *Education Through Community Organizations,* San Francisco, Jossey-Bass, 1990.

Gerard Casey: *Born Alive: The Legal Status of the Unborn Child in England and the U. S. A.* Barry Rose Law Publishers Limited, 2005.

Gerard Casey: *Born Alive: The Legal Status of the Unborn Child in England and the U. S. A.* Barry Rose Law Publishers Limited, 2005.

Harris, John and Soren Holm (eds.). *The Future of Human Reproduction: Ethics, Choice, and Regulation.* New York: Oxford University Press, 2000.

Johnson, R.K.: *The Second Language Curriculum,* New York, Cambridge University Press, 1989.

Kean, N.P. and Breo, D.L., *The Surrogate Mother, Everest House,* New York (1981)

Layne, Linda, *Transformative Motherhood: On Giving and Getting in a Consumer Culture,* New York University Press, New York (1999)

Lovett, T. : *Adult Education, Community Development and the Working Class,* London, Ward Lock, 1975.

Ludden, David : *Peasant History in South India,* Princeton, Princeton University Press, 1985.

Okech, J.G.; Asiachi, A.J. : *Curriculum Development for Schools,* Nairobi, Educational Research Publications, 1992.

Perkins, Roberta: *Working Girls: Prostitutes, their Life and Social Control,* Canberra, Australian Institute of Criminology, 1991.

Rajbhandari, Renu: *Girl Trafficking: the Hidden Grief in Himalayas,* Kathmandu, Naveen Press, 1997.

Ryan, Maura A. *Ethics and Economics of Assisted Reproduction: The Cost of Longing.* Washington, D.C.: Georgetown University Press, 2003.

Sitaramayya, B. Pattabhi : *History of the Indian National Congress,* Bombay, Padma, 1947.

Stuhmcke, Anita, *Surrogate Motherhood: Law and Legislation,* Murdoch University, Australia (1995)

Thomas, A. : *Educating Children at Home,* London, Cassell, 1998.

Vincent, Rose : *The French in India: From Diamond Traders to Sanskrit Scholars,* Bombay, Popular Prakashan, 1990.

Yeaxlee, B. : *Lifelong Education, A Sketch of the Range and Significance of the Adult Education Movement,* London, Cassell and Company, 1929

Index

❑❑❑

www.ingramcontent.com/pod-product-compliance
Ingram Content Group UK Ltd.
Pitfield, Milton Keynes, MK11 3LW, UK
UKHW022122051026
15623UKWH00009B/1187/J

9 789380 920771